YOUNG MAN WITH A RE

YOUNG MAN WITH A RED TIE

A Memoir of Mandela and the Failed Revolution, 1960–1963

Bob Hepple

Bob Hepple

This edition first published by Jacana Media (Pty) Ltd in 2013

10 Orange Street
Sunnyside
Auckland Park 2092
South Africa
(+27 11) 628-3200
www.jacana.co.za

ISBN 978-1-4314-0784-2

Cover design by publicide
Set in Ehrhardt 12/16.5 pt
Printed and bound by Ultra Litho (Pty) Ltd, Johannesburg
Job no. 001980

See a complete list of Jacana titles at www.jacana.co.za

'I dreamed I saw a land. And on the hills walked brave women and brave men, hand in hand. And they looked into each other's eyes, and they were not afraid.'

(Olive Schreiner, *Three Dreams in a Desert*, 1891)

To my family and all the friends with whom I have shared that dream

Contents

Abbreviations

ANC	African National Congress
ANCYL	African National Congress Youth League
APLA	Azanian People's Liberation Army
ARM	African Resistance Movement
BOSS	Bureau of State Security
CIA	Central Intelligence Agency (US government)
CPSA	Communist Party of South Africa (1921–50)
ERRC	European Roma Rights Centre
EU	European Union
FEDSAW	Federation of South African Women
IDAF	International Defence and Aid Fund
ILO	International Labour Organisation
LPSA	Liberal Party of South Africa
MK	Umkhonto weSizwe (Spear of the Nation)
NEC	National Executive Committee
NP	National Party
NUSAS	National Union of South African Students
OB	Ossewa-Brandwag (Oxwagon Sentinel)
PAC	Pan Africanist Congress
SACOD	South African Congress of Democrats

SACP	South African Communist Party (from 1953)
SACPO	South African Coloured People's Organisation; later, Coloured People's Congress (CPC)
SACTU	South African Congress of Trade Unions
SAIC	South African Indian Congress
SALP	South African Labour Party
SLA	Students' Liberal Association
SRC	Students' Representative Council
TIC	Transvaal Indian Congress
TRC	Truth and Reconciliation Commission
UP	United Party

PROLOGUE
23 November 1963

'Kennedy assassinated.' I see the poster as our car pulls up at a red light. I lean out of a window and buy the newspaper from a seller weaving dangerously between the vehicles. For a few minutes all six of us in the car are agog with the news of the shooting in Dallas, Texas. It happened at 12.30 pm the previous day, 7.30 pm in Johannesburg. News takes time to reach us; there is no rolling TV or radio news, indeed no TV at all in South Africa. Dallas is far away, and we are preoccupied.

We are heading for the Bechuanaland border, 260 kilometres away, so that Shirley and I can make our escape from the country. Bechuanaland, a large, sparsely populated, undeveloped country, most of it covered by the Kalahari Desert, is a British Protectorate. A barbed-wire fence that runs for hundreds of miles marks the border with South Africa. There are heavily guarded police posts where roads cross the border. Patrols go frequently up and down the dusty dirt track alongside the fence. We have to find a way over the fence without being spotted by the police or caught and handed over to them by one of the white farmers in the vicinity. We are fearful that even if we get into Bechuanaland, the South African security police will kidnap us and take us back to prison. That has been the fate of some other refugees who escaped into the British Protectorates.

We hope that the Protectorate police will grant us safe passage so that we can make our way to Tanganyika, but there is a risk that we'll be sent straight back.

The driver of the large old Pontiac is Suliman ('Babla') Saloojee, whom I have known as a comrade in the Congress movement for more than 10 years – a fearless, fast-talking, quick-witted man in his thirties, usually full of fun. He gained fame in the 1950s as one of the 'Picasso club', a group of young Indians who painted political slogans at night. One of these, on the walls of the racially segregated Johannesburg Public Library, read 'We Black Folks Ain't Reading'. As soon as the authorities laboriously sandblasted this, a second slogan appeared: 'We Black Folks Ain't Reading Yet!' But today Babla is deeply serious, concentrating on the task in hand.

That task is to help me escape from the 'Rivonia' trial of Mandela and nine others, all of us facing the death penalty on charges of conspiracy to commit acts of sabotage with the intent to overthrow the apartheid regime. I was arrested at Lilliesleaf Farm, Rivonia, the secret headquarters of the underground Congress leaders, while attending a meeting with five of them on 11 July 1963. I was detained and interrogated in solitary confinement for 90 days and then indicted with Nelson Mandela and others. On 30 October the state prosecutor, Dr Percy Yutar, withdrew all charges against me but wants to call me as a witness for the prosecution. I have no intention of testifying against the defendants, whom I admire and respect.

I am 29 years old, practising as an advocate at the Johannesburg Bar. Shirley and I are active supporters of the liberation movement. We were married in July 1960 and have two small children, Brenda, aged two-and-a-half, and Paul, 11 months. From the moment I was released from prison Shirley has recognised that we will both have to leave the country. If I leave without her she will be detained in solitary confinement as a hostage and put under unbearable pressure, as had happened to the wives of other escapees. So she has the cruel dilemma of either being separated from the children by being detained in solitary confinement without trial or being separated from them by coming with me. The choice is clear: she will have to accompany me. We cannot expose the children to the risks of escape. The day before we leave, we meet my parents and Shirley's parents and tell them our plans. We are fortunate in both coming from politically progressive families. It goes without saying that they will take care of the children and bring them to us in England as soon as possible. Early on the Saturday morning we leave the baby Paul with Gertrude Tshabangu, our home help, who thinks we are going to do the Saturday shopping. We take Brenda, a bright lively child, to her grandparents. She waves to us as we drive away, trusting that we will return soon. The grandparents are to tell the police that we had said we were going for a weekend break to a resort near Rustenburg, a town in the western Transvaal. We are using my father's car, which we leave in a car park in the city for him to pick up later. Our own car is still parked outside our house. Later, the police tell the grandparents that they had been watching the house: 'We don't know how they got away – their car was parked outside the whole weekend!'

With Babla in the car is the bearded middle-aged Maulvi Cachalia, in his attire as a Muslim priest. He is a leading member of the Transvaal Indian Congress (TIC), a participant in the 1946 Passive Resistance Campaign, and deputy volunteer-in-chief (Mandela was volunteer-in-chief) in the Defiance Campaign Against Unjust Laws in 1952. I don't know him well but am impressed that he has come along, despite the enormous risks to himself, to help us get away. He is reserved and says little, apart from the occasional humorous remark to relax the tension we all feel. I discover that he and Babla run the 'freedom transport', the escape route that has successfully got a number of other refugees out of the country. They are well organised, efficient and highly secretive. There are two other passengers, Ebrahim Desai and an African whom I don't know at all. They are also political activists trying to leave the country but it is better not to ask why, in case we are arrested and interrogated. Babla says that if the police stop us, we should leave the talking to him. He will say that Maulvi is going to give his advice, as their priest, to a Muslim family and he has asked me to accompany him because there are some legal issues.

Shirley and I sit on the back seat with Maulvi, the other two are in the front with Babla. I am wearing a tweed jacket, grey flannel trousers, white shirt and tie – so I can pass myself off, if questioned, as being on professional legal business. Nine years earlier *Die Vaderland*, a pro-government newspaper, described me as *''n jong man met 'n rooi das'* (a young man with a red tie), the perfectly accurate innuendo being that I have leftist, anti-white-supremacy sympathies. This time I leave the red tie at home and wear a dull striped one. Shirley is a bright-eyed young woman, a head shorter than me, with striking auburn hair. She is wearing a non-crease white dress with a blue floral pattern. She has a vanity case, and I am carrying a small holdall with a change of underwear and a spare shirt.

Whenever Babla notices what might be a policeman or police vehicle he warns us to keep our heads down – two whites in a car full of Asians will arouse suspicion – and there are frequent glances behind to make sure that we are not being followed. He decides to take us to the border through Mafeking, still the administrative capital of the Bechuanaland Protectorate although on the South African side. I can't avoid mentioning to the others the irony that my maternal grandfather, Alexander Zwarenstein, who emigrated to South Africa from Holland in 1898, was a *rapportryer* (dispatch rider) for the Boers during the historic 217-day (October 1899 to May 1900) siege of Mafeking. Now his grandson is using the town as a springboard to escape the Boers, the oppressive Nationalist government of the Republic.

We are soon on the dirt track near the border fence. It is late afternoon and still light. We approach some vegetation by a dried-out riverbed. There is a *kraal* (small village) divided by the fence, half in the Protectorate and half in the Republic, one of those arbitrary demarcations imposed by colonialists on the local people when they were dispossessed. Only now does Babla reveal that our way across will be over a ladder that the villagers have set up to visit the other side. The police know about the crossing and so make frequent swoops in the area. We shall have to trust the local people not to disclose our presence, and hope that the ladder has not been removed. We are told to head for a trading post on the other side, where comrades will be waiting to pick us up in a green Land Rover.

Babla stops the car so that we can get out. With his engine idling he watches us walk the few hundred metres to the village. We are anxious because we can see a cloud of dust less than a mile away down the track. It must be a police patrol. We urge Babla to leave, but he hovers about to make sure we are moving in the right direction. The going is tough through thorn bushes, which tear our clothes, and we have to walk up and down *dongas* (ditches). Now the fears that have been with me for years really kick in. There have been the fears of police raids when we hold secret meetings, fears of arrest as I transport Mandela and other underground leaders around the country, fears of further indefinite detention without trial in solitary confinement with psychological and physical torture, fears of the death penalty which the Rivonia defendants are facing, fears for the welfare of Shirley and my family. But now I have the fear of one who is running away, leaving his comrades and family, facing the dangers of being captured and 'disappearing', or being shot 'while trying to escape'. Most painful of all is the fear of never seeing our children again. Shirley puts on a brave face, but I know that her heart is breaking.

The thoughts of home and children have to be shut out now so we can concentrate on crossing over the fence. We do so watched by some boys playing with a ball. The hand-made wooden ladder is sturdy. Shirley is first over, followed by me carrying the holdall, then our two companions. As we step into the other half of the kraal, on the Protectorate side, we appreciate that we are now fugitives and that we may never again see the country we love. All we have of our worldly goods is one small bag and some photographs of the children.

We walk up the slope towards a trading post. We see two men coming out and, at first, fear they are policemen. Then, as they see us approach, they raise their clenched right fists with thumbs up in the ANC salute. We are overjoyed to see the familiar face of Fish Keitseng. He is the ANC representative in Bechuanaland, a veteran of the Defiance Campaign and Treason Trial, who now organises the escape route for refugees. He escorts us to the Land Rover, tells us to lie down on the back floor and covers us with a blanket. He does not want the Bechuanaland authorities to know where and when we have crossed over; the route must be kept safe for others. There is a bumpy drive along a dirt road into Lobatse, a town of two streets, only one of them tarred for a short distance, that meet to form a T at the railway station. We have to wait on the floor of the vehicle for nearly two hours until it gets dark. We are tired, uncomfortable, desperate to use a toilet, and still scared. After what seems like a very long time we are smuggled with our heads covered into a house occupied by an African couple and their family. Our presence must be kept secret for at least 24 hours. We do not know the couple, but they greet us warmly, offer us food and vacate their bed for us. We protest that this is not necessary, but they insist.

I write a letter to my parents dated Sunday 24 November, knowing that the security police will open it. It is intended to provide evidence that our parents did not know our plans:

> We are sorry we had to mislead you when we asked you to look after the kids for the weekend but we felt it would be inadvisable to tell you anything in advance.

The letter goes on to give some instructions about our personal affairs, and ends

> Kiss the babies for us. We are missing them terribly. Once again – sorry to do this to you. We love you all very dearly and you are always in our thoughts.

We stay in the house until Monday morning when Fish takes us to report to the district commissioner's office, a Victorian building with the Union Jack flying above. The Lobatse officials are inquisitive but polite; they fingerprint us, take our photographs, and want to know where and when we entered the territory. Following Fish's instructions we say that it was dark and we don't know the place we crossed over or the time. The police are not satisfied with this but, no doubt used to this kind of response, they don't press the point. They are keen for us to leave as soon as we can.

We immediately set about finding a charter plane to take us to

Mbeya in southern Tanganyika. The flight will be across white-ruled Northern Rhodesia (later Zambia), whose police would not hesitate to return us to South Africa if we landed. I become nervous when the Afrikaner pilot informs us that he was once a mercenary for Moïse Tshombe, the hated Congolese politician regarded as complicit in the murder of Patrice Lumumba. My anxiety is magnified when I recall that the plane carrying Dag Hammarskjöld, the UN secretary-general, had crashed in mysterious circumstances near Ndola, Northern Rhodesia in September 1961 and Tshombe's secessionists were rumoured to be responsible. (In 1998, Archbishop Desmond Tutu, chair of the South African Truth and Reconciliation Commission, revealed that letters had been uncovered that implicated the UK's MI5, the American CIA and the South African intelligence services in the crash.)

In the small six-seater plane we are joined by the two men who escaped with us. A much-relieved district commissioner sees us off. Soon after take-off from the landing strip at Lobatse, I am alarmed to hear the pilot radio Johannesburg air traffic control to get a weather forecast and tell them our position. I am now convinced that he is going to return us to South Africa or land in Rhodesia. But he does not. We must assume, however, that the message has alerted the South African police that we are making our way to Tanganyika. The pilot insists that Shirley should sit alongside him, with me and our companions behind. He starts to harass her, but stops doing so when she vomits – probably a reaction to the movement of the plane as well as her revulsion.

The pilot tells us that he does not have enough fuel for the whole flight and must land for the night in Kasane, a small place on the north-eastern corner of Bechuanaland, on the south bank of the Chobe River near its confluence with the Zambezi. This is the point where the four corners of Bechuanaland (later

Botswana), South-West Africa's Caprivi Strip (then under South African control, but later part of Namibia), Southern Rhodesia (later Zimbabwe) and Northern Rhodesia meet. We fly over large herds of elephants crossing the swamps. On landing, the local police tell us that our lives are in danger. A refugee plane and the landing strip were sabotaged on a recent occasion. There are South African security agents and their sympathisers in Kasane, and they know we are here. We are advised to stay in the police cells. We go to the local hotel, where the pilot is staying, to buy some food and drink to take back to the jail, and are aware of the hostile looks we get from white staff and visitors. We spend an anxious, sleepless night in the cells. Lying on a blanket on the stone floor I am troubled by this reminder of my recent imprisonment in Pretoria, but this time the cell door remains open and Shirley is beside me.

At first light we are told that elephants have trodden over the rain-sodden airstrip, leaving it unusable, and that the plane has been damaged, although it is not clear whether this is due to marauding animals or hostile agents. We have to wait several hours before the strip is made good and the plane is safe to take off. We then fly at low altitudes over Northern Rhodesia and into Tanganyika. The pilot skilfully weaves the plane in a thunderstorm through the valleys between the high mountains that surround Mbeya. For us it is a terrifying experience, and we are relieved to make a safe but bumpy landing. After reporting to the local district governor's office, we go to a small hotel. At last we feel safe, but we realise that our ordeal is not yet over: the children are still in South Africa and we do not know whether they will be allowed out of the country to join us.

Two days later we make our way to Dar es Salaam (which means 'Haven of Peace') and are warmly welcomed. The ANC arrange for us to stay in the apartment of Frene Ginwala while she is away. We are awoken each morning by the call to prayer from the nearby mosque. We become friendly with Eleanor and Ronnie Kasrils, who have also recently escaped by the same route from South Africa. Eleanor gives a dress to Shirley, who still has only the clothes in which she left South Africa. I have a linen suit made for £1 by a same-day-service Indian tailor. It is an unbearably humid but beautiful city. We are fascinated by the harbour with dhows from Zanzibar and the Persian Gulf, the Arab traders selling carpets on the pavements, the Swahili vendors selling tropical fruits, and the tall Masai people trading artefacts. We make a day trip to the Spice Island, Zanzibar, soon to be united with Tanganyika in the Republic of Tanzania, and are entranced by the Arab architecture and narrow alleyways.

We apply for political asylum to the Tanganyikan authorities. At the Department of Home Affairs, we are interviewed separately. A polite civil servant first asks for my full name, names of parents, place of birth. Then he asks 'Tribe?' I reply, 'I have no tribe.' 'Everyone must have a tribe,' he responds. I say 'South African?' 'No, that is your nationality.' 'European?' 'That is too ambiguous.' Then it occurs to me. 'My grandfather was born in Sunderland. They call those people "Geordies".' The official beams: 'That's good, so your tribe is "Geordie"!' When Shirley's turn comes he is content to accept 'Jewish' as her tribe.

There is, however, no question of us wanting to stay in Dar. It would be impossible to get the children there. We need to get to England if we are to have any hope of being reunited with them. The *Sunday Nation* interviews Shirley while we are visiting my cousin in Nairobi: 'I am very anxious to hear about my children. Paul will be celebrating his first birthday on 11 December. I do not know how it will be, but I hope to have him with us for this occasion.' She says that since leaving home 10 days earlier we have not heard a single word about the children. 'We are trying hard to make contact with them.'

We manage to arrange a flight to London, where we arrive on the cold wintry Sunday morning of 8 December, just two weeks after we left South Africa, freezing in our summer clothes. We are treated as aliens because South Africa has left the Commonwealth. The immigration officer asks, 'What is the purpose of your visit?' I say that I want to study at the London School of Economics. I cannot produce any proof of acceptance by that institution. I then claim political asylum, but a deportation order is served on us, and we are sent to a small waiting room with renewed anxieties. Does this mean they will put us back on a plane to Dar, or maybe even to South Africa? Will we be detained in a prison while they decide what to do? Fortunately, we get a message through to Mannie Brown, a Congress comrade who is waiting to meet us, with two other close friends. The ever-resourceful Mannie manages to contact Canon John Collins, a friend of my father and founder of the Defence and Aid Fund. Our escape is international news, the United Nations has called for the immediate release of all those arrested at Lilliesleaf, and the world press is waiting to interview us. Collins contacts the Home Office, which authorises our admission initially for seven days. After a few hours' delay we leave the airport to stay with an old friend in Hampstead. A week later we are interviewed at the Home Office, helped by the civil liberties solicitor Ben Birnberg, who has eased the passage of many refugees. The Home Office official (I suspect MI5) has a sign on his desk, no doubt intended to be humorous: 'Power is delightful, absolute power is absolutely delightful.' He seems to know as much about me as the South African security police, if not more, and one must assume collaboration between these countries at a time when South Africa is regarded as an ally in the Cold War. Shirley and I are granted indefinite leave to remain. (Three years later we were registered as UK citizens, by virtue of my paternal grandfather's birth in Sunderland.) It takes time to arrange for the children to join us. Too late for us to celebrate Paul's first birthday with him, we spend a miserable, lonely Christmas in a hotel in High Wycombe. At the end of December we are joyfully reunited with Brenda and Paul, who are brought to us in London by their grandmother Minnie.

This book is my story of the events leading to our escape and the start of our new life in Britain. We were caught up in the revolution planned by Mandela and his comrades in the period from 1960 to 1963. Though it failed, it was the spark that lit the fire which destroyed white political supremacy and brought democracy and human rights to South Africa 40 years later.

My involvement in this epic struggle was rooted in the experiences of my youth.

Chapter One

RED TIE
1934–60

Bertha's letter

I was born on 11 August 1934 in a South Africa beset by racial bigotry. Two experiences in my early youth shaped the course of my life. They led me to recognise that the Nazi treatment of the Jews and the behaviour of most white South Africans towards black people, both rooted in theories of master races, shared much in common. Jews and other minorities, such as the Roma (Gypsies), were treated as inferior species and were dehumanised by the Nazis. Black South Africans were also treated as racially and intellectually inferior, and subjected to daily humiliation and degradation.

The first formative experience was in August 1945, soon after my eleventh birthday. A letter arrived in Johannesburg from Amsterdam. It was addressed to my mother's family from their cousin Bertha Monasch. Nothing had been heard from her and her parents, Pinas and Hester, since the Nazis occupied the Netherlands in May 1940. Hester was one of nine siblings of my maternal grandfather (*Oupa*), Alexander Zwarenstein, who had migrated to South Africa in 1898. The letter was in Dutch. Cousin Sprientje translated it into English and called the whole family to her mother Gé's house. We sat expectantly around the large table in Gé's dark-panelled, ill-lit dining room, in a gloom that seemed fitting for the occasion.

Sprientje read out Bertha's graphic account of the 'terrible, terrible times' they had endured, the suffering of her septuagenarian parents and Aunt Marie (Mietje), the liquidation of her father's business by the Nazis, and her mother's thoughts of suicide. On 9 October 1942 her parents and Mietje were taken away, pushed like cattle into wagons, 'packed on top of each other' and transported to Westerbork transit camp, where they stayed for three days with 20,000 other Jews, and 'were robbed of all their possessions'. Later Bertha learned that they had been sent to Auschwitz concentration camp. She had received two postcards, scribbled in pencil in her mother's handwriting, and thrown out of the train near Westerbork. The cards were picked up by friendly farmers, as often happened. The last postcard told Bertha that she must keep courage (*moed houden*). The family house had been seized, plundered and sold to a Dutch Nazi who was still collaring the rent in August 1945.

Sprientje, usually rather cold, sharp and distant, was choked with emotion and stopped several times during the reading. I was conscious that my mother and Aunt Dolly were weeping; everyone else was silent and grim-faced. 'Thank God Oupa isn't alive to hear this,' someone said. He had died at his home in Johannesburg in 1942, and so did not learn the terrible fate of his relatives who stayed behind in the southern Netherlands. The Central Database of Shoah Victims' Names (Yad Vashem) shows that Hester, Pinas and Mietje died in Auschwitz on 15 October 1942. Since the journey from Westerbork to Auschwitz took up to three days, they must have been gassed on arrival.

I found it difficult to understand what I had just heard. I lived in a political household where there was frequent talk of the War. Since the liberation of Auschwitz by the Red Army in January 1945, if not before, I had heard of the camps and Nazi atrocities. But this was the first time I linked them to my own family. What was still distant and incomprehensible was made shockingly real a few weeks later, when my mother decided that I should go with her and my father to our local cinema, the Curzon, to watch the gruesome newsreels about the concentration camps. Parents were advised that these films were not suitable for children, but my mother believed that it was her responsibility to let me see them. She knew that she and my father could explain the atrocities to me in the context of centuries of anti-semitism and racist ideologies. She trusted my human instincts of revulsion, and told me about the acts of heroism and defiance by those who resisted the Nazis. She faced the news of the tragedy, as she did all other setbacks, with 'positive thinking', reflected in sayings like '*alles sal regkom*' (everything will come right), 'think you *can* and you *will*', and the first line of Arthur Hugh Clough's poem 'Say not the struggle naught availeth'. This was the rock from which this warm, emotional and passionate woman radiated her love and support for everyone. She invented a family motto: 'Achievement is better than rest'. This never meant personal ambition – she was profoundly modest about her own achievements – but rather that everyone should strive to make the best of their lives and the lives of others, whatever the setbacks and disappointments. The words from Bertha's letter that stayed with me in times of trouble were those of her murdered mother Hester in her last, desperate postcard – *moed houden*.

———

What I saw in the cinema was truly horrific and revolting. There were the piles of skeletal bodies being pushed into pits by bulldozers, dazed emaciated survivors in their striped pyjama suits, huts into which thousands had been squeezed, and the remains of gas chambers and crematoria which the Nazis had tried to destroy before fleeing. Those images never left me. Nor do the thoughts that six million Jews, half a million Roma and many others died for no reason other than racial hatred and crude theories of their racial inferiority; that disabled people were murdered because of extreme eugenicist ideas; and that tens of thousands of prisoners of war and political opponents were tortured, starved and brutally murdered. I came to realise that had my Oupa not emigrated to South Africa, his fate would have been that of his sisters and brother-in-law and the others who remained behind. I would not have existed. Many years later, I read *Heshel's Kingdom*, Dan Jacobson's book about the Lithuanian Jews who were saved from the Holocaust because their parents had emigrated to South Africa. He observed: 'On the one side of the ocean, death. On the other side, life. The gulf between those swallowed by the catastrophe in Europe and those who escaped is unbridgeable.'

Bertha visited South Africa after the War. She told us that being married to a Christian (Jan van Dam) she had been allowed to stay at home until February 1944. Then it was no longer safe and she had survived by hiding in attics, unable to switch on a light or flush the toilet while those hiding her were out of the house. She was fragile and embittered, sarcastic and resentful about those who had not experienced the destruction of their lives. She spoke with hatred of the willing collaborators, Dutch Nazis and Jew hunters, and members of the Jewish Council who accepted the task of selecting those who would be deported. The revelation of what had happened to my relatives was for me the end of innocence.

BERTHA'S LETTER
(translated from Dutch)

Amsterdam, 21 August 1945

Dear Aunt Gé and Sprientje

I shall try to give a résumé of what has happened here and it could fill a book, so I'll have to cut it as short as I can.

It has been terrible, very terrible times and many, many people have received a bad shock, spiritually as well as physically, including those who stayed at home … So much has happened around us, things that a normal brain cannot conceive. And daily lists of people pour in who died in the concentration camps through extermination, ill-treatment and shooting.

The last time I was able to see my parents in Rotterdam was in March 1942. I was there for a week in lovely spring weather and went for a walk with my mother in the country to the lakes of Lillegosberg an hour's journey out of town. She was so happy to be in the open away from worry. My mother looked pale and tired, too much at home and insufficient fresh air. But still she looked far younger than her years [about 70]. My father was snow white, stooped and walked slowly and sat all day staring into space with a cigar in his mouth. A tired old soul and indifferent to life. Besides this he had a rupture and the doctor had forbidden him to walk much. Added to this Aunt Marie [Mietje, a sister of Oupa] came daily with her complaints and troubles and this was depressing for Mother who had more than her share in life to bear. Mother was glad to open her heart to me and then saw me off

5

on the train to Amsterdam. We sat for a while in the station enjoying the sun. I can still remember exactly how she looked that day. I asked myself if this is the last time we would meet and now I believe this to be so ...

By then an order had come [from the Nazis] to liquidate Father's business. In order not to upset me they had told me nothing about it ... My father did not know of the tragedy awaiting him in spite of many warnings. We did not believe events come with such a storm. All that would happen would be to be deprived of his livelihood for a few months and then return to business. It was no use talking to him. My mother was alternately optimistic and pessimistic, but still at the end was seriously considering leaving the gas-jet open. This was told me by neighbours, perhaps that would have been better and it would have saved her from that torture trip. Who knows?

On the night of 8 to 9 October, in the early hours of the morning, they were taken away. A large bus arrived with Aunt Marie already inside and others. All had one suitcase with some warm clothes and provisions. The preceding evening our old neighbour, who was head officer in the police and who had helped them in the past, had warned them that there was a 90% certainty of their being deported. They would have had a chance to get away by fleeing but Father had lost courage and his attitude was completely apathetic. Had there been a ghost of a hope that they were prepared to go 'underground', I would have arranged for friends to fetch them. These friends were prepared to help and their chance of survival was fair. But I knew too well that they would not consider escaping and that Mother would not do this alone, although she was much more sprightly than Father.

They then spent a day and a night along with a mass of thousands of others at the River Maas. After that they and all the others, young and old, healthy and sick, were pushed like cattle into wagons and packed on top of each other. They were transported to Westerbork near Assen in the province of Drente. By then there were 20,000 people herded together in barracks, along the roads in wind and storm and mainly without food. There they stayed for three days, don't ask how, and then robbed of all their personal possessions, transported in a train to an unknown destination ... Later I heard from an old school friend who managed to have a word with them that the train went to Auschwitz just past the Polish border at Katowice. The train was guarded by the Grüne Polizei who had to leave it eight kilometres before reaching Auschwitz. Thereafter the train command was taken over by SS [Schutzstaffel] troops. In Auschwitz there were enormous concentration camps. Even the guards did not know what would happen next. Directly after arrival, the people were divided into two groups – one left, the other right. All the old and helpless went direct to the gas chambers. The young and workable ones were made to work until they also collapsed. I have accurate information about these facts from friends who managed to escape from this hell ...

*I received two postcards, scribbled in pencil in the train, in my mother's handwriting. It was thrown out of the train near Westerbork and picked up and posted by friendly farmers. This was often done. The last postcard said they were on a journey and the destination was unknown and several other relatives and friends and I must not fret and should keep courage [*Ik moet maar niet treuren en moed houden*]...*

Our house was sealed by the Sicherheitspolizei the

> *same night of my parents' departure and weeks after it*
> *was plundered. Everything the old people had worked and*
> *sweated for their whole life was dragged out ... [T]he house*
> *was bought by a Dutch Nazi who still collars the rent ...*
>   *Many families have been completely wiped out ...*
> Bertha

Diepkloof and the shantytowns

The second experience that led me to make a connection between what had happened in Europe and white domination in South Africa occurred a few weeks after the reading of Bertha's letter. My mother's sister Dolly took me with a group of white high school students on a visit they were making to Diepkloof Reformatory for black juvenile delinquents and the nearby rapidly growing black shantytownships on the outskirts of Johannesburg.

With their love of children, it is no surprise that both my mother and Dolly became primary school teachers. Dolly was regarded as the 'brains' of the family – 'the cleverest girl in the class' – the first family member to attend university (Witwatersrand). Under the discriminatory rules then in force my mother had to resign as a permanent teacher when she married in 1931. Perhaps the main reason that Dolly never married was that she could not face the prospect of sacrificing the work with children that was the centre of her life. I became the child she never had; I called her 'my other mother'. The schools at which she taught were segregated for whites only (this was so even before official apartheid), but she had a deep love of humanity and knew no racial barriers in her dealings with others. She was one of a small group of enthusiastic pioneers of night schools for Africans, who were deprived of the education whites enjoyed. These pioneers were, she wrote in an article in the *Transvaal Education News*, 'aflame with passion to wage unrelenting war on illiteracy', believing that the 'education of our African people is necessary and important if we are to maintain justice and freedom in South Africa'. On 30 September 1940, the Mayibuye Night School for Adult Africans opened its doors in the rooms of an African trade union in Kruis Street, central Johannesburg. (*Mayibuye iAfrika*, an African National Congress [ANC] slogan, means 'Come back, Africa'.) Dolly was one of the organisers and teachers. There were many obstacles to overcome – cramped and noisy space, insufficient tables and benches, lack of resources such as blackboards and books, and overwhelming numbers of would-be learners shared among a handful of teachers. Despite the difficulties, branches were opened in other areas. By 1941 there were so many requests that they decided to take pupils as far as Junior Certificate (eight years' schooling) and enter them for public examinations. The Mayibuye school was allowed by the then principal to use Ferreirastown Indian Government School in Market Square, a school of which Dolly's uncle, Solly Zwarenstein, had once been principal. I sometimes went to the adult classes with her and, although still a schoolboy, helped to teach basic literacy to these students, much older than myself. Another development was that white high school students, inspired by the Mayibuye project, started community literacy projects for Africans; by 1945 Dolly could report that at least 19 organisations were teaching more than 1200 adult Africans, but even this could not meet the growing demand.

It was with a group of these white students, all older than me, that I visited first the Diepkloof Reformatory, and then the townships. The reformatory had been transformed by Alan Paton (principal from 1935 to 1948, and later the courageous leader of the Liberal Party) from a barbaric detention centre into a modern penal institution in which the emphasis was on education and rehabilitation. Having never been inside a prison before, I was shaken by the dark, cold punishment cells and the disciplined regime.

Large numbers of starving Africans were moving in from the countryside seeking work. They were living in the areas of Moroka and Jabavu in hessian and corrugated-iron shacks, with no electricity, no running water, and open sewers. I saw ill-clad children with bare feet and potbellies caused by malnutrition. It was a shock for a boy who lived in Kensington, an all-white residential suburb 32 kilometres away, in a brick house with an iron roof and an extensive cultivated garden and orchard, who travelled on whites-only trams, and who went to an all-white school. I met black people only as domestic servants or as workers in the family's wholesale meat factory. White South Africans nearly always had black domestic servants, usually living in a small room in the backyard.

When my parents got married, Oupa sent one of his workers, Frans, to help them. They decided that it was demeaning to ask anyone to live like that, so they turned to daily helps. For over 30 years, Lizzie came every week to do the washing and ironing, and her sister Alice came to clean the house. Lizzie and Alice had to travel the long journey on crowded commuter trains from Orlando township, but at least they could live with their own families. As their political lives became busier, my parents needed more help, so they employed a 16-year-old Bavenda called Wilson. I was about 12 at the time. I taught him to read and write. I was an only child and he was often my sole company, but in those days there could never be the friendship of equals. Like the white schoolboy in Athol Fugard's evocative play *Master Harold and the Boys*, I would always be the 'young master' and he would be the 'boy'. Living in a room in the backyard, he had to face the harassment of night raids by the police looking for those who had no permission to be in a white area, and he had to be given a 'special' pass by us to go out after 10 pm. I remember how, one 'Dingane's Day' (16 December, when Afrikaners celebrated the Boer victory over the Zulus at Blood River in 1838), I found Wilson lying injured in the street. He had been severely assaulted by young white thugs shouting that he was a *kaffer* [a derogatory term for an African] who should keep off the streets.

This connection between Nazism and white domination was reinforced for me when the National Party (NP) and their Afrikaner Party allies narrowly won the white general election in 1948. My mother wept when she heard the result. I could not understand why she was so upset, because we were at the same time celebrating the election of my father as a Member of Parliament for the Rosettenville constituency representing the Labour Party, which had an electoral pact with General Smuts's United Party. She explained: 'These people supported Hitler and will do what the Nazis did.' My parents were not only active in the Labour Party but were also members of the small but vocal anti-fascist movement. They spoke of the similarities between the master-race ideology of the Nazis and the policies of white domination in South Africa. During the War my father volunteered to work at night as a member of the Civilian Protective Services (a kind of 'Dad's Army') to relieve younger men fighting at the front in North Africa and Italy. While engaged on these duties, he was severely assaulted one night by members of the Ossewa-Brandwag (OB), a militant national-socialist movement which sought the establishment of an authoritarian state with citizenship confined to 'assimilable white elements'. The links between the OB and the National

Party were strong. Among its members were John Vorster, later National Party prime minister; Hendrik van den Bergh, later head of the South African Police Security Branch and the notorious Bureau of State Security (BOSS); and Oswald Pirow, later prosecutor in the Treason Trial against ANC leaders. In May 1945, my father prophetically asked in the *Labour Bulletin*: 'After years of sacrifice and bitter struggle against fascism abroad, must the future South Africa breed a nation of bullies, persecutors and terrorists and provide new Buchenwalds?' When Mosley, leader of the British fascists, established links with Pirow, my father wrote: '[White] domination is not possible under democracy, but offers great possibilities to those who put their faith in fascism.'

Understanding racial oppression

I became deeply aware that the worst thing you can do to another human being is to treat them as a mere object. It was the single-minded lack of empathy of the Nazis for the Jews and other minorities that led to the Holocaust. A similar lack of feeling of many white South Africans for their black compatriots underpinned white supremacy in South Africa. In his last book, *The Drowned and the Saved*, Primo Levi, the Italian author and survivor of Auschwitz, eloquently explains the difficulty of drawing a clear line between the victims and their persecutors ('the grey zone'), and the way in which persecutors in all ages hold on to power by binding some of their adversaries with the burdens of guilt and blood, compromising them as much as possible. When asked why there were no large-scale revolts by deported Jews, Levi responded that there were indeed some who did rebel, knowing that they were going to die one way or another, such as a group of 400 Jews from Corfu in 1944. Prisoners who had just got off trains, dishevelled, dirty and hungry after days standing in cattle trucks, were led to believe that they were queuing for showers and did not realise that gas chambers awaited them; if they showed the slightest sign of knowing their fate, the guards used extreme brutality to keep them in line. Levi says that the Jewish prisoners were, for the most part, devoid of any kind of organisational or military experience and were in such a state of degradation after years of starvation and persecution in ghettos that revolt was not feasible. Anne Frank's biographer Melissa Müller comments: 'The Nazis knew how to strip people of their self-worth. They knew how to bring people to the point at which they would just give up.'

The maintenance of a system of racial superiority requires a long period of demonisation and dehumanisation of the 'other'. In Germany the idea that Jews were an inferior racial species, and were responsible for Germany's defeat in the First World War as well as the subsequent woes of the Weimar Republic, had become part of the popular culture. There had been a long cultivation of the pseudo-science of 'racial hygiene'. Nazi propaganda portrayed Jews as malevolent Bolsheviks and hereditary criminals. Traditional anti-semitism was carried to extreme lengths. How was it possible for this to happen in a highly educated country, the heart of European culture, the birthplace of Heine, Mendelssohn and Einstein? After the War, many Germans said that they did not know that millions of humans had been exterminated in gas ovens. I heard a similar defence of ignorance from white South Africans after the fall of apartheid. One notorious 'hanging' judge said to me in 1990: 'I just did not know that the security police were torturing and killing suspects.' One has to ask, how was it possible for millions to be deported in Europe, and thousands of protesters to be fired upon, detained without trial and tortured in South

Africa, without anyone's knowledge? Despite extensive media censorship, it was not possible to conceal the reality of torture, murder and forced evictions. As a non-political South African cousin admitted to me: 'We did not want to know.' There were also those who claimed they were compelled to carry out orders, regardless of their content. This does not explain the acts of extreme cruelty that went beyond 'orders'. In South Africa, no one was compelled to be a security police officer, and when it came to compulsory military service there were many draft resisters. Just as Hitler had 'willing executioners', so the majority of the white population in South Africa were complicit in the cruelty and suffering caused by apartheid. They found it difficult to avoid the peer pressure, of the kind I described earlier, to treat black people as inferiors who were to be feared. But there was always a minority, including my parents, who joined the ranks of the resisters.

In my case, it was the opportunity to meet black people as equals at university and in the Congress movement that shaped my attitudes. This was reinforced when, at the age of 19, I went with a group of friends on a 10-day hike over the Drakensberg mountains into the Kingdom of Lesotho, led by Eli Weinberg, a communist who earned a living as a photographer after he was banned by the government from his job as a trade union official. We stayed with Basotho peasants and learned about their lives. Despite the absence of formal education they were articulate, intelligent and mature. I appreciated then that all human beings are, in the words of the first article of the Universal Declaration of Human Rights, 'born free and equal in dignity and rights'. The attitude of many whites, however, was reflected in the remarks of an Afrikaner who gave us a lift on the back of his truck while we were hiking. When we told him we were heading into the mountains, he said, *'Daar is geen mense daar, net kaffers'*

(There are no people there, only kaffirs). He described how he went on raids in the area with the police trying to stop *dagga* (marijuana) smuggling, and it was considered 'fair game' to rape the women.

School days

My developing attitudes to racism put me out of step with my schoolmates and most of my teachers. Jeppe High School for Boys, which I attended from 1947 to 1951, was a selective-entry whites-only state school modelled on English grammar schools of the early 20th century. In the tradition of those schools, violence was endemic. The boys were regularly beaten by teachers and prefects for any of a variety of misdemeanours. Some used a cane; others were content with a ruler. One of the teachers wielded a short *sjambok* (hide whip); and the rugby coach 'sliced' boys' bottoms with the long metal chain of his whistle on cold afternoons while they were in shorts. I nearly always avoided the humiliation of a beating by being quiet in class, arriving on time, doing my homework and listening to the coach.

My school reports recorded that I was 'hardworking' and 'steady', nearly always at or near the top of my class, and I matriculated with distinctions in my two favourite subjects, Latin and history. Had I achieved a predicted distinction in mathematics I might have become a land surveyor because, as an urban boy, I longed for the outdoor life. But my activities in the debating and dramatic societies, and keen interest in politics and law, attracted me instead to a career either as a journalist or an advocate.

The whole school system was based on the premise of racial supremacy. After the Nationalists gained power, so-called Christian National education explicitly aimed at cultivating a privileged white elite who would continue to dominate black South Africans. As a school librarian in the fifth form I met with the disapproval and irritation of my English teacher by daring to invite Alan Paton to give a talk on his book *Cry, the Beloved Country* about the tragic lives of Africans coming to the 'City of Gold'. One teacher who did inspire me was Mr Etheridge, a left-of-centre war veteran, who in the fourth form taught the French Revolution and enthused over the ideas of *liberté, égalité, fraternité*. But when I wrote an essay in the fifth form for another teacher, a veteran of the legendary Royal Air Force Pathfinders, quoting with approval Rousseau's dictum 'Man is born free, but everywhere he is in chains', he dubbed me a 'communist'. When I wrote another essay for him on the social consequences of the Industrial Revolution, he threw it back to me across the classroom, saying sarcastically, 'This was written by the Labour Party.' I was disappointed but not surprised that I was not made a school prefect. Perhaps this was because I lacked the sporting talents so highly prized in this school, but I think it more likely that it was because I was regarded as an outsider in the conservative world of white privilege.

There was, however, one experience that changed my perspectives and showed me a different world outside the narrow, prejudiced confines of white South Africa. In 1949, when I was 14, my parents let me join a three-month trip of 56 boys from the school to Britain, France and Switzerland. It was led by the kind and caring Mr Luckin and his lively wife, also a teacher at the school. My diary of this trip reveals my excitement at seeing 'the lovely green countryside' of Hampshire, marvelling at history being brought alive in castles and cathedrals, being shocked by the devastation of war around St Paul's Cathedral which stood splendidly alone on Ludgate Hill, being disgusted by the industrial haze of smoke over the slums of a 'very dirty'

Birmingham, laughing at the *pissoirs* in the streets of Paris, and being excited by my first sight of snow on the mountains in Switzerland. After this visit my reading shifted from the usual boys' adventure stories of Empire and white conquest, such as those written by H Rider Haggard, Percy FitzPatrick and Rudyard Kipling, to books about Europe, the rise of fascism and the struggles for equality and socialism. In my late teens I started to read the great 19th-century Russian novels by Tolstoy, Dostoevsky and others, which helped me to understand how events in society can affect ordinary lives and relationships and how one has to find one's own path to freedom.

Radical university student

A new world opened for me when I entered Witwatersrand University (Wits) in 1952. I immediately joined the Students' Liberal Association (SLA). This broad left organisation had been set up after the Nationalist election victory in 1948 to oppose racial discrimination in the academic sphere and to engage students in the political situation in the country. At SLA meetings there were vigorous debates about how best to resist apartheid and establish a democratic society. The frequently rowdy arguments reflected the ideological divisions between liberals and radicals, the latter including socialists, communists and Trotskyites. While the liberals saw the issues almost entirely within the perspectives of white society, and advocated 'dignified', non-political and symbolic protests, the radicals' view was that only by an alliance with the black majority, which meant in practice the ANC, could the Nationalist plans for university apartheid be halted or delayed. The dominant figure in the SLA at the time I joined was Harold Wolpe, a communist who continued to be actively involved in politicising students after he left the university in 1952. He later achieved celebrity status for his escape with Arthur Goldreich following the Lilliesleaf arrests. He had a somewhat aloof and remote attitude to younger students, but he loved a good intellectual argument and had a neat turn of phrase. When the Pan Africanists and Trotskyites argued against alliances with liberals, he called for a united front, using the analogy of a long journey: 'We're all on the same train but some will get off before others!'

The struggles outside the university constantly impinged on our academic discussions. In August 1952, two black medical students, Diliza Mji, the president of the ANC Youth League (ANCYL), and Nthato Harrison Motlana, secretary of the League, were arrested at the Medical School, as part of the police action to break the Defiance Campaign. I joined about 250 other students in a protest march, organised by the SLA, from the university gates to the magistrates' court to participate in a large demonstration when Mji and Motlana were charged alongside 19 other Defiance Campaign leaders, including Mandela, with offences under the Suppression of Communism Act. I was full of admiration for two white students, Margaret Holt and Sydney Shall, who took part in the Defiance Campaign. Sydney, a medical student and one of the accused in the 1956 Treason Trial, and Joan Anderson, a fellow member of the SLA and Congress movement, became my closest friends, with whom every issue was discussed.

The greatest excitement of those days was the spirit of comradeship, of hope, of invulnerability, that I found among the group of like-minded liberal and leftist friends. Most of them were white, but since Wits was an 'open' university, for the first time in my life I also met Africans and Indians as equals. After a boys-only school, I enjoyed the company of progressive young women. It felt like bliss to be alive. To be young, on the left, and sometimes in love was, to recall Wordsworth, 'very heaven'. I revelled in the hours sitting in the student café with liberals, socialists and communists, debating the issues of the day, and exploring with new friends the hidden haunts of Sophiatown and the Indian restaurants and shops around Market Street in central Johannesburg.

In April 1954, aged 19, I emerged into the limelight after being arrested for breaking a petty apartheid law and spending a night in the cells. I was one of 22 whites, mainly students, who had entered Orlando township to put on a concert for location residents. We were participating in the 'Transvaal Youth Festival', which had the subversive slogan 'Peace, Friendship and Racial Harmony'. One of those arrested paid the £10 fine for entering without a permit; the rest of us, in a spirit of defiance, refused to do so. At the first hearing, the magistrate said he accepted we had no ulterior motive. But he was wrong in this, and the security police knew it. Although we had been in the township for only three hours, they raised the charge to the absurd one of 'illegal squatting', which carried a prison sentence rather than a small fine. This was designed to frighten others who dared to challenge petty apartheid. Some of us were already members of the South African Congress of Democrats (SACOD), an ally of the ANC, and the concert was really a cover for a political meeting. We had persuaded a few budding performers in the student dramatic society to join us. We had to attend court over several weeks as the case dragged on, but at the end we were all acquitted. It was on this occasion that *Die Vaderland* (Fatherland), a pro-government newspaper, reported that *''n jong man met 'rooi das'* (a young man with a red tie), referring to me, had given evidence. I must have worn the tie deliberately – I felt really proud! I had stepped out of the shadow of my father, who was well known as leader of the Labour Party. Our lawyer was Harry Bloom, who later acquired fame as the author of *Transvaal Episode*, one of the first novels about black township life, and of the book for the musical *King Kong*. (Twenty years later he and I became colleagues at the University of Kent at Canterbury.) The experience of the arrests had a lasting impact. Some of the 22 were chastened and melted away. A few of us were hardened in our resolve to fight against apartheid and ended up a few years later in prison or exile.

The publicity surrounding the case did me no harm among the student body. I was already a member of the Students' Representative Council (SRC), elected on the SLA 'ticket', and was elected president in 1954. The issue that dominated student politics was discrimination against African, Indian and Chinese students – collectively referred to as 'non-Europeans'. Wits and the University of Cape Town (UCT) were the only 'open' universities that did not exclude non-Europeans. In practice, there were very few: by 1952, out of a student population of about 4000 there were only 245 non-Europeans at Wits and only 298 in 1959. The Nationalist government had declared that it would introduce racial segregation in the universities. Liberal and radical students were united in their defence of what was called 'academic non-segregation'. However, the University Council, while purporting to preserve the status quo, submitted to government pressure on vital issues. It imposed a quota on the number of black medical students. At the end of the same year, following the student protests against the arrest of Defiance Campaign leaders, the principal issued a remarkable statement on students and politics in which he said that the students' actions and policies were bringing the university into disrepute and that the SRC was 'unrepresentative' of the student body.

The university also succumbed to attacks by government ministers that there was no social segregation at Wits and that 'white girls went about with "kaffirs"'. The University Council decided to impose racially segregated seating in the Great Hall of the university, which had traditionally been non-segregated. In response a mass meeting of students decided to boycott the hall for all segregated functions and directed student clubs and societies to follow this decision. When the Choral Society defied this democratic decision in order to perform Gilbert and Sullivan's *Ruddigore* (we called it 'Ruddybore'), the SRC withdrew recognition and financial support from the society and organised a demonstration. As an organiser of that demonstration, I was summoned on 28 May 1954 to the office of Professor Sutton, the new principal, and informed that if I organised or participated in such a demonstration I would face expulsion from the university. My friends and I ignored the warning. On the opening night, the hall was half empty with only a few students in the audience. We put up a banner in front of the main entrance, and during the interval we showered the audience with protest leaflets as they entered the foyer.

Sutton took no further action against us individually, but with the backing of the University Council he suspended the SRC constitution and assumed powers to veto the SRC's actions. He was an arch-conservative, and was determined to crack down on the radicals whom he and the Council blamed for involving the university in politics. He disliked the leftists for what he described as the 'utter cheek' they displayed towards the authorities. The historian of the university, Bruce Murray, interviewed Sutton after his retirement. Sutton claimed that on one occasion he had rebuked me: 'You are giving me lip.' I supposedly retorted: 'I have been mandated to give you lip.' That was not my style of negotiation, but Sutton's memory of the incident is indicative of the atmosphere between him and student leaders like myself. Under my presidency in 1954–5 of the SRC, the last elected under the old system, we waged a sustained campaign to block the adoption and implementation of the new imposed constitution. Over 2000 students (half the student body) signed a petition for submission to Parliament. At a mass protest rally a manifesto of student rights was adopted. But the Council went ahead and dissolved the old SRC on 15 August 1955. My colleagues and I decided not to cooperate in handing over our assets to the new SRC. We argued long and hard over whether those of us who had condemned the new SRC as a puppet of the authorities should participate in the new arrangements. We decided to do so for fear of losing a platform among the students but emphasised that in doing so we were not 'condoning' the new SRC. At the same time we set up a Witwatersrand University Students' Association to defend the rights of students. The authorities banned us from operating on campus, so we had to hold elections on a piece of land outside the main gates. The Association soon faded away.

The new SRC was elected under a system designed to weaken the radicals. For the first time since 1945 there was no African on the SRC, and there was at first only one woman. The radicals had gained a majority on the old SRC by concentrating their efforts on a few faculties, such as arts, where they had most support. The new electoral system of proportional representation on a university-wide basis for most of the seats meant that we also had to garner support in the conservative faculties like engineering. Despite this, several radicals, including Ismail Mahomed (later first black chief justice in democratic South Africa), Sydney Shall and myself, were elected, but overall control passed to the liberals. The left had been marginalised on the SRC, and most of its leaders either joined the overseas brain drain or devoted themselves to their careers. A few moved towards revolutionary politics outside the universities. No doubt it had been naïve for the radicals to believe that they could move white students closer to the demands of the black majority for equal rights, but we did have significant support, as shown by the 2000 signatures on the petition and the election of several radicals to the new SRC. The emasculation of the SRC made it easier to impose segregation on the universities. Sutton, backed by a conservative Council, behaved dismally by turning his guns on the radicals in the SRC rather than the Nationalist government.

Congress of Democrats

Outside the university, I came to meet leaders of the Congress movement with whom my life was bound up for the next nine years. Ruth First described me at a public meeting we both addressed in a Fordsburg cinema in 1954 as a 'promising young leader'. Ruth was charismatic, always handsomely attired, and had a brilliant mind and sharp tongue, so I was chuffed by her praise. Knowing of my interest in journalism, she soon involved me in writing for *New Age*, of which she was Johannesburg editor, and the journal *Fighting Talk*. I also spent a vacation working for the trade union newspaper *Saamtrek* and learned how to subedit from Dawie Couzyn, the energetic young Afrikaner editor. This stood me in good stead when I became a co-editor of *Wits Student* and, a few years later, co-editor with Leon Levy of *Workers' Unity*, the Congress trade union newspaper.

It was a natural progression from student politics for me to become chair of the youth branch of SACOD, small enough to meet regularly in the unpretentious flat in Wolmarans Street of two older members, Alan and Beate Lipman. SACOD had been formed in 1953 as an ally of the ANC. Its main aim was to persuade the white population that their long-term interests lay in equal rights for all. It differed from the Liberal Party in two main respects. First, SACOD adopted a policy of votes for all without any qualifications; the Liberal Party advocated a non-racial franchise restricted to those with suitable educational or property qualifications. Second, although in theory membership of SACOD was open to all races, in practice it restricted its membership to white people so as to avoid competition with the ANC, the Indian Congress and the Coloured People's Congress. It was the 'white' voice within the multi-racial Congress alliance; the Liberal Party opened its doors to all races, in direct competition with the congresses. Like many radicals, I did not like the racialisation of the Congress movement but I appreciated that it was important not to undermine the ANC, the principal opposition to white domination. Underlying the policy differences was the Cold War, then at its height, and the deep hostility of some liberals towards the communists, who were the dominant influence in SACOD. The communists did not help matters by taking decisions on SACOD activities within the Communist Party, excluding prominent non-communists such as Helen Joseph and Len Lee-Warden from having a say in these decisions. SACOD was vocal but had little, if any, impact on white people.

For me the importance of SACOD was the opportunity it gave to 'connect' with the masses. Every Friday night several of us went down to the bus queues to sell *New Age* to Africans as they waited to catch their crowded buses back to the squalor of Alexandra township. The queues were notorious for muggings and stabbings, especially on Friday, which was payday. The waiting black passengers were astonished to see young whites ducking and weaving among them, apparently impervious to these dangers and to the risk of arrest. But we never experienced hostility and sometimes there were animated discussions about the news and views in *New Age*. We got to hear first hand about people's grievances.

Labour Party

Why did I not join the Labour Party when I reached adulthood? My grandfather Tom Hepple, an active trade unionist, and his wife Agnes Borland, a suffragette, were founding members of the South African Labour Party, a party of white mainly English-speaking workers, in 1908. My father Alex and mother Girlie devoted their lives to the Labour Party. I have told their story in a biography, *Alex Hepple: South African Socialist* (2011). Their socialist beliefs made the Labour Party a natural home. It was the English-speaking white community in which Alex had grown up and he knew many of the Labour leaders and members as family friends. My father and mother believed that the best role they could play was as a bridge between black and white by persuading their colleagues in the Labour Party and the white electorate to accept the inevitability of majority rule.

My childhood and youth were dominated by their activities. I was wheeled in my pram and later walked on my own young feet at countless Labour Party conferences and political demonstrations with my parents. I participated in my father's election campaigns, which were meticulously organised by my mother, and sat in awe in the parliamentary gallery as he delivered some of his most telling attacks on the Nationalist government. I treasured the days when we debated the big questions at the family dinner table, and when I walked around the golf course or climbed Table Mountain with him. He had the gift of giving straight and uncomplicated explanations, and was patient with others less clear-sighted than himself. He was undemonstrative and had simple, conservative tastes, worked hard but enjoyed his golf and always found time for me. When he was elected in 1948 to Parliament, which sat in Cape Town, my mother decided to accompany him because she was able to leave me in our own home with her sister Dolly for those six months each year. This

25

lasted for 10 years until he lost his seat in 1958.

Under my father's leadership after 1953, the Party moved away from its earlier policy of 'communal representation' of 'non-Europeans' in the white Parliament, towards the objective of universal adult suffrage and the ending of the exclusion of non-Europeans from Parliament. Moreover, while neither the Liberal Party nor SACOD had clear economic policies, the Labour Party, like its British counterpart, had the objective of a planned, democratic socialist society based on the common ownership of the means of production, distribution and exchange. (The Freedom Charter, which SACOD but not the Liberal Party endorsed in 1955, had only an ambiguous commitment to 'the mineral wealth beneath the soil, the banks and monopoly industry' being 'transferred to the ownership of the people as a whole'.) The Labour perception of 'equality of opportunity' went beyond the Liberal one. It was not limited to removing distinctions based on a person's race or gender, but it coupled the principle of 'equal pay for equal work' with the removal of all disadvantages that black workers suffered in the labour market through discrimination and inferior treatment. The Labour Party's membership was in practice limited to white people, but since I accepted SACOD's reasons for the organisational tactic of de facto racial divisions, I could hardly object to this.

My real problem with Labour was that it was a purely parliamentary party with an ageing and declining membership, and with parliamentary representation only so long as it had electoral agreements with the supine white-supremacist United Party. By 1958 it had been eliminated from Parliament and ceased public activities. My university friends were moving either into the Liberal Party or SACOD. When my parents decided in the 1930s to devote themselves to Labour, it had been a thriving party built around first- and second-generation

English immigrants. It was boosted by Labour's success in Britain in 1945. By 1953, the English-speaking working class was being overtaken by a growing class of Afrikaner workers who had been indoctrinated by the Nationalists to support extreme racial policies.

Communist Party

The only party that had members of all races on the basis of equality, and had socialist objectives, was the Communist Party. But that party had dissolved itself in 1950 shortly before being made illegal. As a teenager, I was inspired by *News from Nowhere*, William Morris's dream vision of England transformed into a 'socialist commonwealth', with no class conflict or national boundaries, men and women living as equals in harmony and freedom, production for use and not profit, and the abolition of prisons and other machinery of state oppression. It was only when I started reading some of the Marxist works on my father's bookshelves that I came to believe that socialism was not only realisable but also inevitable. My parents' generation of socialists – influenced by Fabians such as Bernard Shaw, and Sidney and Beatrice Webb – saw the Soviet Union as the world's first socialist state, a 'new civilisation'. Marxism attracted me because of its social and economic optimism. A brief visit to the Soviet Union in August 1954, to attend an international student conference as the delegate of the National Union of South African Students (NUSAS), led me to admire what my guides showed me of the achievements of 'socialism' in industrialising a formerly backward country. I was not then aware of the starvation and violence that had accompanied collectivisation, or of Stalin's great purges. I was, however, troubled by the reluctance of our Soviet guides to answer questions frankly. For example, an enquiry as to why Beria, one of the leaders, had been summarily executed was met with a chilling stare and the statement that he was 'an enemy of the people'. My disillusion with 'really existing socialism' came later. The watershed for me was the Soviet invasion of Hungary and Khrushchev's famous 'secret' denunciation of Stalin at the 20th Congress of the Communist Party of the Soviet Union in 1956. After that, nothing could be taken on trust from the Soviet leaders. But things looked differently in the early 1950s. I can remember a fellow student breaking down in tears in 1953 when he conveyed the news that Stalin had died. Most of the Jews from Russia and the Baltic states who formed the core of communist sympathisers in South Africa dismissed reports of Stalin's terror as 'capitalist propaganda', and refused to believe the authenticity of the reports of Khrushchev's speech.

On my father's advice that one could not understand politics without mastering economics, I took economics as a three-year major subject in my first degree. Works by Marx and Marxists were not on the official reading list, and were banned by the government's Publications Board. This enhanced their allure – if they were dangerous enough to be feared by a reactionary government, they must have something to teach us. Our academic teachers were contemptuous of Marxist ideas. Professor Ludwig Lachmann, head of the economics department, was a follower of Friedrich Hayek long before his neo-liberal ideas became popular. My friend Charles Feinstein's dissertation for his honours degree, which advanced claims for Marx's labour theory of value and drew some political implications from this, was rejected by the external examiner, Professor WH Hutt of the University of Cape Town, and he was advised that he would do better submitting the essay to Moscow University! Encouraged by Maurice Dobb, the Marxist economist, Charles went to Cambridge in October 1954; we later became colleagues at Clare College. In 1989, he was elected Chichele Professor of Economic History and Fellow of All Souls College, Oxford.

At the time, Marx seemed to many radicals like myself to offer a 'scientific' solution to South Africa's twin problems of racial domination and economic exploitation. Marxists such as Harold Wolpe argued that apartheid – like earlier forms of white supremacy – was designed to serve the interests of the dominant capitalist class and was the means by which capitalism could achieve rapid economic growth. 'Cheap' African labour was seen as essential to the maintenance of the rate of profit – the survival of capitalism and of apartheid were thus interlinked. Liberal economists, on the other hand, saw apartheid as primarily an ideological phenomenon that was irrational and inimical to economic growth. In the 1950s and 1960s, the Marxist view seemed highly plausible. It was only later that clear evidence became available showing that South Africa's worsening economic performance was in large part a consequence of apartheid policies constraining the growth of manufacturing and the domestic market. 'Cheap' labour in fact undermined the growth of productivity. Apartheid had become a fetter on capitalist development, not its facilitator. What we failed to appreciate – as did most Marxists at the time – was capitalism's enormous capacity for survival, innovation and adaptation with or without racial domination.

Those who wanted to explore Marxism had to do so secretly. It was in June 1954 while attending a small group reading Engels's *Anti-Dühring* that I was taken outside by Wolpe and asked if I knew that the Communist Party had been secretly revived. No, I did not, although I suspected this. Would I be interested in joining? Yes, I would. Here, I thought, was a party in which I could be an equal member with people of all races working towards socialism. I would become an 'insider', no longer on the white fringes of the movement. I was assigned to a unit with three other university students, an Indian and two whites. One of them was the contact with Wolpe, who was at the next level of Party organisation. The only people we knew as Party members were those in our own unit.

I was soon disillusioned. The Party engaged in no independent activities whatsoever. It was a secret conspiratorial group, and it was a serious breach of discipline even to expose the existence of the Party to any person who was not known to be a member. As far as the public was concerned there was no Communist Party in existence. There were debates from time to time as to whether the Party should 'emerge'. The objections to emergence were always on a practical rather than political level. The first was that it was necessary to prepare the Party's allies for this event, so as not to lose their cooperation, bearing in mind that an open association with an illegal organisation might compromise the legal status of the ANC. Secondly, it was said that the South African Communist Party (SACP) was not prepared organisationally to withstand the attacks from its enemies that would inevitably follow emergence. I became aware, towards the end of 1955, of a decision to emerge. Wolpe introduced me to Michael Harmel, who told me he was a member of the Central Committee. I was going to London on a student travel bursary, and he asked me to take a manifesto of the Party, which was to be printed in England, and then shipped to South Africa for mass distribution. I hid the document in the lining of my suitcase, and then handed it to Vella Pillay of the London bureau of the Party. We discussed a plan to ship the printed copies back to South Africa. When I returned home in January 1956 I learned that the operation had been stopped. Moses Kotane, the general secretary, had been advised to delay emergence by communist leaders while on a visit to the German

Democratic Republic. I was never told the reasons for this.

The unit structure made it impossible for individual members to know what the majority of members felt on particular issues. There were secret Party conferences from time to time, of which units were informed, but the Central Committee handpicked the delegates. I discovered through indiscreet conversations with presumed Party members that there was widespread dissatisfaction and frustration with the inertia of the Party leadership and their isolation from day-to-day struggles. They were described as crocodiles that slept in the sun and snapped only when anyone moved! This had led to the growth of informal factions and some expulsions. There was also disintegration within the Party organisation. I was told that Party units in some areas had fallen apart well before 1960 because they found their meetings a waste of time. My own unit simply stopped meeting some time in 1956 and lost touch with the Party. No effort was made to revive it.

I was disaffected with the Party for several reasons, including the failure to have an in-depth discussion of a strategy for emergence as an independent party, the kowtowing of the Central Committee to the Moscow line on the invasion of Hungary, the authoritarian methods of the leadership and their support for the Soviet Communist Party despite Khrushchev's revelations at the 20th Congress about Stalin, and the 'cult of personality'. I was frustrated by the isolation of the small 'family' of white communists, concentrated in the north-western suburbs of Johannesburg, from the black communists and other activists in the south-western townships. This was perhaps inevitable as racial segregation became stricter and meetings between black and white became increasingly dangerous and difficult. The black trade unions offered greater opportunities for a white person to meet and work among black people, although this too was not without its difficulties. I decided to devote myself to union work. There was no procedure for formal resignation, but I simply dropped out of the Party after 1956. I was to reconnect with the remnants of the organisation in 1960 during the exceptional circumstances of the state of emergency, when the very survival of the extra-parliamentary opposition was threatened. After three years of intensive activity, I finally parted ways with the Party in 1963.

In 1956 I was a second-year law student, working during the day as an articled clerk in an attorney's office, going to night school at Wits University, and spending most evenings and weekends in the law library. I graduated with distinction in 1957 and was awarded the Society of Advocates Prize as best law graduate. So there was not much time for political activity until 1958 when I qualified as an attorney and went to work for my cousin Fred in the firm of Edelson and Zwarenstein. I did not enjoy their largely criminal law practice – Fred told me that I lacked the 'killer instinct' necessary to become a great defence advocate like Vernon Berrangé – and wanted more time for my activities in helping the black trade unions. I was then co-editing *Workers' Unity*, organ of the South African Congress of Trade Unions (SACTU), giving free legal advice to the struggling unions, and conducting study groups of black trade unionists in places such as Iscor (the Iron and Steel Corporation). In January 1959 I took a job as a lecturer in law at Wits University, which left me with more time for these activities.

Then, on 21 March 1960, came the Sharpeville massacre, followed by spontaneous uprisings, the banning of the ANC and other organisations, the state of emergency, and the move towards armed struggle. Nelson Mandela emerged as the most prominent leader of this new phase of the struggle. My life became increasingly bound up with his.

Chapter Two

STRUGGLE ON, MANDELA!
1960–62

Young Mandela

There is a sculpture of Nelson Mandela in Parliament Square, London, unveiled in 2007, that portrays a kindly old man bending slightly forward with open welcoming arms, a furrowed brow, narrowing eyes and a mouth opening as if to speak words of comfort. That is not the 34-year-old Mandela I first saw in 1953. The sculpture represents the icon, an almost mythological character. It is the image of the man the world wants him to be – the great redeemer who emerged from 27 years of imprisonment filled with forgiveness and the spirit of reconciliation. But such a person could not have survived the brutality of Robben Island. Nor could he have been the hard-headed professional revolutionary who sacrificed everything to lead the armed struggle against the apartheid regime: his career as a lawyer, his children, and Winnie, the woman with whom he was passionately in love and whom he had married in June 1958.

It was at a public meeting on 28 June 1953 at the Odin Cinema, Sophiatown, that I caught my first glimpse of Mandela. This tall, good-looking, charismatic young man had sprung to national attention the previous year as volunteer-in-chief of the ANC's Defiance Campaign. He, Walter Sisulu and other colleagues in the ANC Youth League were in the process of turning the rather moderate and elitist ANC into a militant mass movement, and were willing to use strikes, boycotts and civil disobedience. Mandela already had a reputation as a hot-blooded critic of the older conservative leadership of the ANC, and he was hostile to what he then saw as the undue influence of white communists on the ANC. I was a 19-year-old pro-ANC student activist, one of a handful of whites at the lively, exuberant meeting among a sea of about 1200 black protesters. This was one of my first experiences of a demonstration of this kind, mixing as an equal with black and mixed-race residents of Sophiatown and their supporters. They were demonstrating against the white government's intention to forcibly remove families who had lived in the area for generations, and to re-zone it for whites only. I was conscious of the black audience's curiosity at seeing some young whites in their midst, and also of the hostility and contempt for us of the white police.

The banning orders that prohibited Mandela and Sisulu from attending gatherings had expired just a few days before the meeting. Word got around the excited audience that they were going to speak. But the police were determined to prevent this. Major Prinsloo and armed officers stormed into the meeting and dragged Yusuf Cachalia of the Indian Congress, who had begun to speak, off the platform. We all began yelling and booing. Things were looking ugly. The next we knew was that Mandela had jumped onto the platform and started singing a protest song. We all joined in. His presence of mind, pulling the crowd into a disciplined peaceful response, had calmed the people down and prevented what could have turned into a riot and shooting by the police.

It was his quick thinking, calm authority, almost serenity in the face of danger, which impressed me most on that occasion.

A little later, at one of the protest meetings in Freedom Square, Sophiatown, I heard a speech by Mandela – which he has described in his autobiography as 'rabble-rousing' – stating for the first time in public, that passive resistance could never overthrow a white minority regime intent on retaining power, and that violence was the only weapon that could destroy apartheid. For Mandela, *satyagraha* – the Gandhian ideal of changing your enemies' hearts and minds by peaceful passive resistance – was never a principle, but only a tactic that had been tried and failed. His speeches were, however, rarely emotional and were never scintillating. In a deep, resonant voice, speaking slowly and deliberately, choosing his words carefully, and in a stiff style, he would appeal to reason from a deep sense of conviction of the justice of his cause.

The young Mandela had the reputation of being a 'man about town' who liked women, and women were attracted to him – 'N[elson] gorgeous' recorded his friend Mary Benson in her diary when he visited her in London in 1962. He was six foot two, and had the superb physique of a boxer – he was himself a keen amateur boxer and enjoyed watching and talking about the sport. He would excitedly recount how he had watched 'Greb' Mtimkulu floor the legendary 'King Kong' in the third round of their fight. He worked out daily. While he was living under cover in 'safe' houses, he would get up at 4.30 am each day and do at least 90 minutes' exercise.

He took good care of his appearance, wearing a thin moustache just above his upper lip, which reminded me of Errol Flynn, the dashing Hollywood actor. Shortly before going underground he started to grow a beard, which grew bushier when he disappeared from public view, but this could not disguise the high forehead, full cheeks, penetrating eyes and wide, slightly mischievous smile that marked him out among other men. He was a smart dresser, wearing tailor-made three-piece suits in court and at public meetings. He enjoyed eating in the few good restaurants that admitted Africans, but he disapproved of excessive drinking – I recall an occasion when he was furious with two comrades who were late for a meeting because they were inebriated, and he gave us all a short lecture on the need to discipline those guilty of alcohol and drug abuse. He enjoyed township jazz and the singing of freedom songs. I saw him laughing and excited, as he sat in the Wits University Great Hall in February 1959, on the opening night of the all-African jazz opera, *King Kong*. His friend Todd Matshikiza composed it and another friend, Nathan Mdledle, played the title role of a prize fighter, with Miriam Makeba in the role of Joyce, a shebeen queen. On some of our car journeys while he was underground we would sing together 'Sad times, bad times' with its haunting refrain 'What have these men done that they should be destroyed?'

Black Pimpernel

My first personal contact with Mandela did not occur until December 1960 at a secret conference. I had the task of making the practical arrangements for the meeting, attended by about 25 people. I rented a furnished house in the white Johannesburg suburb of Emmarentia and stayed in it with Shirley so as to give the appearance of a normal occupancy. The house was in a secluded garden in which I put up a marquee because the building was not large enough for all to sleep indoors. I hired a closed van, picked up the delegates at various prearranged points in the city and took them in and out of the grounds by night. I noticed the thinly disguised Mandela climb into the van. When we arrived at the house, he shook my hand warmly, and asked, 'How are your parents?' He knew them well because my father, Alex Hepple, was chairman of the Treason Trial Defence Fund and, as leader of the Labour Party, was seen as the voice of the voteless black majority in the white Parliament. At the end of the conference, when I returned him to central Johannesburg, Mandela gave me a big smile and handshake and said, 'You kept us all safe – well done!' It was the beginning of a personal relationship of trust that developed over the next three years.

The repeated banning orders, trials and detention kept him out of public activities. On 29 March 1961 the Treason Trial, which had been running since 1956, ended with the acquittal of Mandela and all the other accused. Encouraged by his close comrade Walter Sisulu, Mandela decided that he would have to go underground, defying the banning orders and evading the police, in order to give effective leadership to the three-day stay-at-home that was planned for the end of May in protest against the declaration of a white republic that excluded the majority of the population. He also wanted to make preparations for the new phase of armed struggle. When he went underground, I was asked to join a support team in Johannesburg that moved him around safe houses, took him to secret meetings and carried messages. Since a white man would arouse suspicion if seen with a black passenger, Mandela would don a cap and white chauffeur's coat and drive my smart green Wolseley car, with me in the back seat. We were never stopped, but there could be embarrassing situations. Once, while driving to pick him up from the house of a sympathetic doctor in Norwood, where he was living in the servants' quarters posing as a gardener, I observed a car that seemed to be following me. I kept stopping, hoping it would go away. Then I noticed that the driver was my friend Albie Sachs, on a visit from Cape Town, who had seen me and wanted to say hello. I got out of my car and said to him, 'Bugger off, Albie.' He looked startled, but realised that something was going on and disappeared.

Mandela coped with the challenge of functioning in hiding with enormous self-discipline and optimism. I usually found him relaxed and in good humour, and never appearing to be nervous, but it was clear that he was missing Winnie and would speak emotionally when expressing his concerns about her wellbeing. Wolfie Kodesh, the cheerful, resourceful *New Age* journalist who, with Ahmed Kathrada, took the primary responsibility for Mandela's safety, managed to arrange some risky conjugal visits. But there were long periods when Mandela was alone, unable to move during daylight hours outside Kodesh's apartment in Yeoville, or the house in Norwood or, from October 1961, Lilliesleaf Farm in Rivonia. He occupied himself with exercise, reading, and making extensive notes. He read voraciously, in particular works on armed liberation struggles, ranging from Clausewitz's *On War* to Mao Zedong and Edgar Snow on China, Menachem Begin on Israel, Che Guevara on Cuba, and Deneys Reitz' classic *Commando* about the Boer War.

In this period, I was struck by Mandela's natural charm and ability to treat everyone as an equal. Some biographers speak of his 'aloofness', but that is not how I knew him. On a few occasions I smuggled him through the back door into my house in Victory Park for a meeting. He would immediately go up to Gertrude Tshabangu, our home help, greet her in her native Setswana, ask after her family, and joke about these white people for whom she was working. When she brought us tea he would include her in the casual conversation. That was something many of our white leftist visitors did not do. He knew that he could rely on her discretion. Whenever he met me he exuded a sense of warmth and concern. His first words were 'How is your family?' Then he wanted to know what I was doing, my latest case or my activity in the trade unions, and he was hungry for world and local news.

Sydney Kentridge, who acted as one of the defence advocates in the Treason Trial, observed that Mandela had emerged from that trial as 'a natural leader of men. He was firm, courageous, [his actions] always based on thought and reason.' In working with him I came to admire these qualities but also sensed an element of bravado. He understood the feelings of ordinary people and could respond to them as occasion demanded, becoming a symbol of defiance and willingness to sacrifice all for the cause of his people. His optimism inspired others, but it also made him vulnerable. His attitude to his own security was almost careless and infected with romanticism. He revelled in being dubbed the 'Black Pimpernel' – like Baroness Orczy's elusive Scarlet Pimpernel, 'we seek him here, we seek him there, [they] seek him everywhere.' He took huge risks and felt the need to keep a revealing diary and notes of his activities as well as his extensive reading on guerrilla warfare, which were later used as part of the evidence to condemn him to life imprisonment.

He ignored the warnings to take care when he visited the province of Natal in August 1962, after his return from an extended trip around Africa to gather support for the armed struggle. He not only exposed himself to too many people in Natal – including Bruno Mtolo, who later turned up as 'Mr X', the chief state witness in the Rivonia Trial – but he even attended a large social gathering. On Sunday 5 August, travelling in a conspicuous new car with the well-known theatrical producer Cecil Williams, he was arrested at Howick on his way back to Johannesburg. Some biographers have detected a wish for martyrdom in his apparently rash indifference to being captured. But he was not an immature, ignorant Joan of Arc claiming divine will for his cause. He was a man of action, impatient to awaken the sleeping giant of his people's anger and frustration with white domination. His attitude was 'who dares, wins'.

Black man in the white man's court

I was shocked and upset to hear the news of Mandela's arrest, although it had been half expected ever since his return from abroad. At this time I was practising as an advocate at the Johannesburg Bar. I was in close touch with advocate Joe Slovo, a leading communist and co-founder with Mandela of Umkhonto weSizwe (MK), the Spear of the Nation, the ANC's armed wing. Slovo, an ebullient, risk-taking and optimistic revolutionary, told me that there were plans for Mandela to escape from prison, but these came to nothing. I later learned from Mandela that he had considered the plans seriously, and had smuggled out a sketch of the prison, including the prison hospital, where he was being lodged by a friendly commanding officer. However, he had ruled out an escape attempt at that time because the high degree of police vigilance while he was awaiting trial made it likely to end as a dangerous fiasco. Meanwhile, a public 'Free Mandela' campaign was launched under the leadership of Ahmed Kathrada, who was soon placed under house arrest and confined to his tiny flat in Johannesburg.

There were two charges against Mandela. The first was that between 1 April and 31 May 1961 he had incited workers to stay away from work illegally as a means of protesting against the (apartheid) laws. The second charge was that he had left the country without a valid passport for his visit to other African countries. The trial was set down for hearing in the Johannesburg Regional Magistrate's Court on 15 October 1962. At the last moment, on Saturday 13 October, he was moved to Pretoria and his attorney, Harold Wolpe, was informed that the attorney-general had directed that the venue of the trial would be a special Regional Magistrate's Court in the Old Synagogue, Pretoria, which had been converted a few years earlier into a courtroom for the Treason Trial. The government was plainly trying to avoid a large demonstration by supporters. Moreover, Slovo, who had been briefed as counsel, was restricted by a banning order to the magisterial district of Johannesburg. Mandela was granted a postponement for one week. Mandela was proud to admit that he had organised the stay-at-home by way of protest against a law which neither he nor his people had any say in making, and he also admitted that he had no passport because the government would not grant him one. He decided to conduct his own defence because, as he told the court, 'this is a case of the aspirations of the African people'. Because the trial would be conducted on a political basis it was obvious that lawyers could not put such a defence forward. The services of counsel were, however, required to assist him with various aspects of the trial. Slovo was initially granted permission by the minister to attend the trial, but as soon as it was discovered on the morning of 22 October that Mandela would conduct his own defence, the permission was withdrawn and Slovo had to return to Johannesburg.

I received a telephone call from Wolpe the same morning, telling me what had happened. 'Nelson wants you to attend the trial as his legal adviser in place of Joe.' I had no hesitation in saying yes, although this meant giving up a remunerative brief to appear in a commercial case. In his memoir, written in prison, Mandela recalls: 'Joe Slovo was replaced by Bob Hepple, a member of the Congress of Democrats and in whom I had the fullest confidence. He was able and dedicated and this made the task of conducting the defence comparatively easy for me.'

I arrived at the Old Synagogue in time for the afternoon session, and went to the room where Mandela was confined. I was taken aback to find him wearing tribal dress, a *kaross* (animal-hide cloak), with a wide bead necklace in the gold, green and black colours of the ANC. I was used to seeing him in court dressed as a lawyer in suit and tie. My reaction was that of a white left-winger who viewed tribal dress with suspicion: this, I thought to myself, is how the Afrikaners want to portray Africans, as still living in a tribal state and not as citizens of a modern, industrial society. Mandela could sense my surprise. He said, 'Winnie brought these for me.' I had already seen Winnie waiting for the case to resume, wearing traditional beaded headdress and an ankle-length Xhosa skirt. A number of ANC supporters in the public gallery and outside were similarly dressed. 'I want our people to see me as a black man in the white man's court,' Mandela said to me. In his autobiography he explained: 'that day I felt myself to be the embodiment of African nationalism ... the *kaross* was also a sign of contempt for white justice.' After I heard his opening application to the magistrate I realised that my instinctive reaction to his dress had been wrong. During the hours that we discussed the case I came to appreciate that Mandela was anxious to embrace the image of a proud African nationalist, to counter the claims of Robert Sobukwe's breakaway Pan Africanist Congress (PAC) that they alone were the true patriots. On his recent trip around Africa Mandela had been alarmed to find that leaders of independence movements in other African countries pictured the ANC as being under the domination of white communists and not as a genuine African organisation.

Ironically, when I had defended Zachius Molete a few months earlier on charges of being an office-bearer of the banned PAC and for furthering PAC activities, he had not refused to recognise the white court, nor played an 'Africanist' card. The prosecution case against him was based on documents he had written and speeches he had made. He was content for me to call Julius Lewin as an expert in African politics to say that, despite the strong anti-white rhetoric, the demands being made could not be described as Pan Africanist objectives. The magistrate found Molete guilty and sentenced him to three years' imprisonment, but I persuaded the appeal court to overturn the conviction on the ground that pursuing these objectives did not prove that he was a member and office-bearer of the organisation. While Molete, a man of considerable intellect and commitment, was willing to play down his membership and to rely on legal technicalities, Mandela opted to use the court as a political platform for African nationalism, regardless of the consequences. Some other ANC defendants followed Mandela's example. When I defended John Gaetsewe, acting general secretary of SACTU, in March 1963 on a charge of illegally leaving South Africa to attend an international trade union conference, he did not deny the charge but refused to recognise any obligation to obey a law which he and other Africans had no voice in making. As he was led away to serve his sentence he raised his fist in the ANC salute.

Mandela and I walked together into the court. There was a large crowd outside and about 300 black spectators in the well of the court and in a segregated section of the upper gallery, with about 50 whites in the other part of the gallery. The black spectators were thrilled by his kaross and defiant manner. They rose as he entered and shouted '*Amandla ngawethu*' (Power is ours; or, Power to the people), and '*Shosholoza* * *Mandela*' (Struggle on, Mandela). Mandela felt that he 'carried into that court the past, the history, the culture and the proud heritage of my people'.

Mandela made an application for the recusal of the senior regional magistrate, Mr WA van Helsdingen, whom he knew from legal practice. Characteristically, he made it clear that there

---

* *Shosholoza* in the Nguni languages is derived from *ishongololo*, which means a centipede. Therefore, the movement of trains that carry miners from their villages to the industrial areas is likened to the movement of the centipede. 'Move forward' or, in this context, 'struggle on' seems an appropriate translation.

was no personal reflection on the magistrate's integrity: 'I hold your Worship in high esteem and do not for one single moment doubt your sense of fairness and justice.' He put forward two grounds for the magistrate to stand down which he knew full well had no legal basis, and which I could not have advanced if I was speaking as counsel. Van Helsdingen tried twice to interrupt him, saying that he was going 'beyond the scope of your application', but Mandela persisted and was allowed to continue. His aim was political, to make it clear from the start of the proceedings that he intended to put the white state on trial. The first ground was that, as a black man, he could not be given a fair trial in a white man's court: 'Why is it that in this courtroom I face a white magistrate, am confronted by a white prosecutor, and [am] escorted into the dock by a white orderly? Can anyone honestly and seriously suggest that in this type of atmosphere the scales of justice are evenly balanced?' The second ground was that he considered himself neither legally nor morally bound to obey laws made by a parliament in which he had no representation. The prosecutor barely bothered to reply, and Mandela's application was summarily dismissed. He had set the tone – white supremacy was on trial. He pleaded not guilty to both charges.

The prosecution called more than 100 witnesses, including policemen, journalists and township officials. Mandela did not dispute the basic facts – he had incited people to join a three-day stay-at-home, and had left the country without a passport. He and I discussed whether and how he should cross-examine any witnesses who might give evidence to support his political case against white supremacy. One of those we lighted on was Mr Barnard, the private secretary to the prime minister, Dr Hendrik Verwoerd, widely regarded as the ideological architect of apartheid. Barnard gave evidence of a letter written to Verwoerd by Mandela, as secretary of the All-in African National Action Council established in Pietermaritzburg on 25 amd 26 March 1961 at a conference attended by 1500 delegates from all over the country. The letter conveyed the demand of the conference that there should be a national convention representative of all South Africans, to draw up a new non-racial democratic constitution, failing which there would be country-wide demonstrations and a stay-at-home would be called for 29, 30 and 31 May. Mandela managed through courteous but persistent cross-examination to get Barnard to concede that the letter raised questions of vital importance to the African people, such as the right to vote and other freedoms that they did not enjoy.

Barnard admitted that the prime minister had not acknowledged the letter but had referred it to the Ministry of Justice – meaning, in effect, to the police. Mandela put it to him that 'in any civilised country in the world it would be at least most scandalous for a Prime Minister to fail to reply to a letter raising vital issues affecting the majority of its citizens'. Barnard did not agree and said it was because of the 'tone' of the letter that there was no acknowledgement. In response to a parliamentary question, Verwoerd said that the letter was 'aggressive'. Mandela then put to the witness a second letter he had written to Verwoerd on 26 June, asserting that the government had sought to suppress the stay-at-home by force. This included mobilising the army, arming European civilians, passing special legislation authorising detention without trial of people organising the action, banning meetings and arresting thousands of Africans under the pass laws. This letter, too, had not been acknowledged. Mandela could claim the moral high ground – the prime minister had not responded to reasonable demands, and peaceful protest had once again been met by state violence. This exposure, Mandela hoped, would help to prepare the people for a new phase of armed resistance.

The evidence of state witnesses also yielded a surprise. On the first day of the stay-at-home, press reports suggested that the turnout was not as good as Mandela and his colleagues had hoped. He confessed that he felt 'let down and disappointed' and that evening told the press that the days of non-violent struggle were over. On the second day, after consulting colleagues, he called off the projected three-day stay-at-home. At his trial 18 months later, state witnesses testified that the stay-at-home had not been a failure – hundreds of thousands of people had not gone to work, the buses transporting workers were empty, and the action had caused great disruption. In the first draft of his closing speech, written before we had heard this evidence, Mandela wrote: 'It has been said that the fact that the strike failed showed that we did not enjoy the support of the people. I deny that.' The final draft has my handwritten amendment (underlined) saying 'At the time the newspapers suggested that the strike was a failure and that we did not enjoy the support of the people. I deny that.' Mandela also agreed to my insertion: 'In any event, the evidence in this case shows that it was a substantial success.' Whether Mandela would have called off the stay-at-home if he had known the true situation in May 1961 remains open to question. The evidence did show that he and his colleagues continued to enjoy widespread mass support despite repression, but his thoughts and actions were all concentrated in preparing for an armed struggle. For him, the stay-at-home, whatever the level of support, marked the end of a chapter of peaceful protest.

Two incidents during the trial illustrate Mandela's most basic quality, his sense of empathy – the ability to identify what another person is thinking or feeling and to respond to their thoughts and feelings with an appropriate reaction. The first is his attitude to Van Helsdingen. Louis Blom-Cooper, an English barrister, was attending the trial as an observer for the human rights organisation Amnesty. Late on the second day he told me that he had seen the magistrate going off in a car for lunch with two Special Branch detectives, one of whom was Detective Warrant Officer Dirker, a state witness, while the other had been assisting the prosecution. I told Mandela that he had good legal grounds for asking Van Helsdingen to recuse himself. Mandela was hesitant. He had refused to recognise the authority of a white magistrate, appointed by a government in which as a black man he had no say. His defence was political and not based on accusations of personal bias. He was worried that an attack on the magistrate's integrity might detract from the political nature of his defence. I argued that an exposure of the cavalier attitude of the magistrate to the ordinary proprieties of a fair trial would support Mandela's case that the white man's court was contemptuous of the rights of a black defendant. Mandela was persuaded by this argument, and decided to make an application for the magistrate's recusal.

But he said to me: 'I have nothing against Van Helsdingen personally, and I do not want to embarrass him. Please go and see him before the hearing resumes and tell him what I am going to do, that it's not meant personally.' I was astounded that he put the feelings of the magistrate who was about to send him to prison above the advantage that he could gain by taking him by surprise in open court. When I carried out my instructions and spoke to Van Helsdingen in his chambers, he went red in the face and spluttered to me that he had not discussed the case with the officers, and that they were merely escorting him for his protection. When Mandela made the application in open court, he emphasised that he had a high regard for the magistrate as a person but added, 'I am left with the substantial fear that justice is being administered in a secret manner.' Van Helsdingen refused to step down and the case continued.

The other incident concerned the prosecutor, Mr JP Bosch. On the morning of the day Mandela was to make his closing speech, we were consulting in his room. There was a knock on the door. It was prosecutor Bosch: 'I'd like a private word with Mandela.' They knew each other from the days when Mandela practised in the Johannesburg Magistrates' Court. 'Don't be crazy,' I said. 'You can't speak to him alone in the middle of a trial.' But Mandela intervened and said he did not mind. He asked me to wait outside. I left them. When Bosch came out of the cell about five minutes later, I saw tears streaming down his face. I asked Mandela: 'What the hell's going on?' He replied: 'You won't believe this but he asked me to forgive him.' I exclaimed, 'Nel, I hope you told him to get stuffed.' To my surprise, Mandela responded: 'No, I did not. I told him I knew he was just doing his job, and thanked him for his good wishes.' In his autobiography Mandela recalls that Bosch said to him: 'I did not want to come to court today. For the first time in my career, I despise what I'm doing. It hurts me that I should be asking the court to send you to prison.' Mandela continues: 'He then reached out and shook my hand and expressed the hope that everything would turn out well for me. I thanked him for his sentiments, and assured him that I would never forget what he had said.' The qualities of understanding and empathy that Mandela displayed during his trial were to stand him in good stead in the 27 long years of his imprisonment and in the negotiations for a democratic South Africa. He also needed the iron will and unshakeable belief in his cause that he displayed when he went underground.

Mandela and I discussed whether he should give evidence. Since the facts were not in dispute and he was obviously going to be found guilty on the two charges, we agreed that there was no point in his doing so. Moreover, the state witnesses did not appear to know that on his African trip he had garnered support for the armed struggle and undergone some military training. If he exposed himself to cross-examination this might give the state evidence that it could use to bring more serious charges at a future date. He closed his case without calling evidence, to the prosecution's surprise. The magistrate adjourned the hearing to 7 November, when he found Mandela guilty on both charges.

Mandela decided to concentrate on a closing speech before sentence was passed. He fully expected to get the maximum sentence on each charge, but the speech would be another opportunity to challenge white supremacy. He prepared a first handwritten draft. I filled in some gaps in information (for example, about massacres of black protesters) and did some editing before having it typed up. We then had a discussion, following which a few passages were deleted and some handwritten amendments made. It covered 32 foolscap pages, and took over an hour to deliver at the adjourned hearing on 7 November. This time the magistrate did not interrupt Mandela. Unfortunately, very little of the speech was published in South Africa, apart from in *New Age*, which was closed down by the regime shortly afterwards. Although general permission had been given to the press to report what banned persons such as Mandela said in court, the government had warned already scared editors 'not to abuse this by creating a forum for such persons' and they were advised that Mandela's speech fell into this category. After the trial, I sent a copy of the speech to England. An edited version was published in *The Observer* and other international papers. Mrs Helen Suzman, the Progressive Party MP, read out part of the speech under the protection of parliamentary privilege and this enabled the *Rand Daily Mail* to report its content. A sympathetic British lawyer wrote to me saying that I must have written it for Mandela. Nothing could be further from the truth. It was his work alone, save for some minor corrections and phrasing from me.

The speech prefigured the more famous statement from the dock that Mandela made in the Rivonia Trial in 1964. There were several themes, the most important of which was that the campaign for a national convention was a 'last attempt to persuade the Government to heed our legitimate claims, and thus to avoid a period of increasing bitterness and hostility and discord in South Africa'. The choice was not between a monarchy and a Voortrekker-type white republic: 'We were inspired by the idea of bringing into being a democratic republic where all South Africans will enjoy human rights without the slightest discrimination.' It was the government that 'had set the scene for violence by relying exclusively on violence with which to answer our people and their demands. Government violence', said Mandela, 'can do only one thing and that is to breed counter-violence amongst the people, till ultimately, if there is no dawning of sanity on the part of the Government – ultimately, the dispute between the Government and my people will finish up being settled in violence and by force.' The battle lines were being drawn for a new phase in the liberation struggle.

Revolutionary leader

The speech also signalled that a new type of leader, a professional revolutionary, had emerged for this new and dangerous phase. Mandela spoke movingly of the sacrifice this involved. Being separated from his wife and children, and taking up the life of a man hunted continuously by the police had not been easy.

This has been a life infinitely more difficult than serving a prison sentence. No man in his right senses would voluntarily choose such a life in preference to one of normal family, social life which exists in every civilised community. But there comes a time, as it came in my life, when a man is denied the right to live a normal life, when he can only live the life of an outlaw because the Government has so decreed to use the law to impose a state of outlawry upon him. I was driven to this situation and I do not regret having taken the decisions that I did take. Other people will be driven in the same way in this country …

The magistrate took 10 minutes to consider the sentence, which was the maximum allowed: a total of five years' imprisonment, three of these for inciting the stay-at-home, and two for leaving the country without a passport. He claimed that Mandela had shown no remorse and that his main objective was to overthrow the government: 'There is no saying how far things will go if they are not put down with a heavy hand.'

I raised the issue of a possible appeal against the severity of the sentence, the stiffest to be imposed in recent times for a political offence, but Mandela immediately rejected this because it would be tantamount to recognising the legitimacy of the white courts. As the court rose, Mandela greeted the crowd with his clenched fist and the *Amandla* salute. The crowd reciprocated with '*Mayibuye iAfrika*' (Let Africa come back). They ignored a prohibition on demonstrations relating to trials and marched through the streets singing '*Amandla ngawethu nobugcwele ngobethu*' (Power to the people, our cause is just), '*Nkosi Sikelel' iAfrika*' (God bless Africa) and '*Shosholoza Mandela*' (Struggle on, Mandela).

51

Mandela was moved, pointing out that the date, 7 November, was an auspicious one, the anniversary of the Bolshevik Revolution. He aimed to continue leading a revolution in South Africa. There were tears in my eyes as he thanked me and we said goodbye and hugged one another. I had been able to tell him that, in response to his arrest, the UN General Assembly had for the first time voted in favour of sanctions against South Africa, and that MK units had carried out acts of sabotage in Port Elizabeth and Durban, celebrating the UN vote and in protest at his trial. We were both optimistic that the struggle would intensify under the leadership of others who would take his place, and that he would soon emerge from imprisonment. We did not foresee the arrests at Lilliesleaf Farm just nine months later, the discovery there of Mandela's diaries and notes, the subsequent Rivonia Trial, and the sentences of life imprisonment on Mandela and on MK's High Command. Nor did I expect to be arrested and detained, and to have to make difficult choices that ended in my escape and exile from South Africa.

Chapter Three

THE RIVONIA RAID
11 July 1963

The illusory 'safe' house

I am full of anxieties as I drive the 25 kilometres from my chambers in central Johannesburg to the meeting at Lilliesleaf Farm. This is a secluded 28-acre smallholding with an attractive modern farmhouse and outbuildings in Rivonia, a peri-urban area in which the wealthy 'mink and manure' set live with their horses and many black servants. The SACP arranged the purchase of Lilliesleaf through a front company in 1961 because it seemed to offer an ideal 'safe house' for those engaged in underground activities. Arthur Goldreich, an artist and industrial designer, and his wife Hazel live in the main house as the nominal occupiers with their two young sons, Nicolas and Paul. A colourful man of the world, Goldreich fought with the Palmach, the leftist military wing of the Jewish National Movement, in Palestine in the 1940s. His connection with the Party and MK, of which he was an early member, is not publicly known, so he and his family provide an ideal cover. The farm workers have been recruited in Sekhukhuneland, an ANC stronghold, and are considered to be discreet and reliable. From October 1961, Mandela lived in hiding in an outbuilding behind the main farmhouse, posing as a gardener, adopting the alias David Motsamayi.

Joe Slovo introduced me to the place after I became one of Mandela's support team in 1961. Sometimes I went on my own to fetch Mandela for meetings in the city or to return him afterwards. After Mandela's arrest, the farm continues to serve as a hiding and meeting place for the underground leaders, who have skipped bail or house arrest. Today I am due to meet four well-known leaders on the run from the police – Walter Sisulu, Govan Mbeki, Raymond Mhlaba and Ahmed ('Kathy') Kathrada – together with Lionel ('Rusty') Bernstein, who is under 12-hour house arrest and must get home by 6 pm in order to comply with his banning order. Together we constitute the secretariat of the Central Committee of the SACP. I am the only one at freedom.

I stop more than once to ensure that I am not being followed. I take a secondary road so as to avoid the Rivonia police station. I am worrying about a mysterious Indian man who came unannounced to my chambers that morning, asking me to convey a message from 'Natalie' to 'Cedric', code names for the Natal district and the central leadership. There is believed to be lax security in Natal. Ever since Mandela's arrest on 5 August 1962 on his way back to Johannesburg from Durban, there are suspicions that the American CIA has given Mandela's whereabouts away in return for the release of one of their operatives who is being held by the security police. Why, and by whom, has the visitor been given my name? I feign ignorance, say I am busy and tell him to come back the next morning. I intend to check his credentials at the meeting.

Another worry is that many arrests have been made, including on 25 June five or six MK trainees who know about the farm. It can only be a matter of time before someone cracks under interrogation and torture and reveals the location of this hiding place. Breaches of security at Lilliesleaf are legion.

Although intended to be used only as a safe house, over time the MK National High Command have taken it over as their headquarters. They bring in trainees, who see the underground leaders living there. The cars of well-known banned people like Slovo, Michael Harmel and Harold Wolpe, whose number plates must be well known to the police, come in and out. (Indeed, it turns out later, in a statement to the police dated 5 August 1963, that George, the 10-year-old son of neighbours who owned a caravan park over the road, often came to play with Nicolas and Paul. He noticed white and black men talking together and shaking hands in the thatched cottage. This seemed strange to him and he told his parents. He wrote down the registration numbers of cars parked in the Goldreich yard and handed them over to the local Rivonia police.) Goldreich invites personal visitors there – one day his cousin bursts into the thatched cottage where we are meeting and is able to have a good look at those present.

Each of these security lapses is criticised, but each time the action of individuals is justified on grounds of expediency. Those – like myself – who visit the farm infrequently, and are not members of MK, become aware of the reckless behaviour of some of the outlaws only second-hand. Unfortunately, some colleagues treat criticisms as personal attacks and as a reflection on their political work. Govan Mbeki reflects the attitude of the outlaws in the remark: 'To hell with the police. If they come we'll shoot it out. I'm not going to prison again.' This is said after a rifle is found under one of the beds – contrary to all the house rules. In his memoir Rusty Bernstein sums up the state of mind of those living at Lilliesleaf: 'In retrospect, it is evident that the "safe house syndrome" was at work. Lilliesleaf Farm seemed to be the easy option for every hard choice. It was, after all, "safe". I began to sense that in the top MK echelons there was a gung-ho spirit of recklessness – though in their perilous cloak-and-dagger operations they would probably have called it a necessary boldness.'

Towards the end of June 1963, after the place has been used for a broadcast from Radio Liberation, it is decided to move out as soon as possible. However, there is always a plausible reason why it is impracticable to do so. Some of the senior leaders are moved to another secret hideout (of which I am unaware) in Travallyn agricultural smallholdings near Krugersdorp. On Saturday 6 July there is a meeting in the main farmhouse to discuss Operation Mayibuye, a plan for launching a full-scale guerrilla war against the apartheid regime. No agreement can be reached and it is decided that the secretariat should meet again on Thursday 11 July to continue the discussion and to deal with some operational matters. The 'accommodation committee', convened by Bram Fischer, has been unable to find another safe house for our meetings. With much misgiving, we all agree that this will be 'the last time' at Lilliesleaf. We ask those who have been living there whether the buildings have been cleared of all incriminating documents. They say that the place is 'clean'.

At about 3 pm on 11 July I approach the main gates of Lilliesleaf. I give way for another car being driven by a white man I do not know who is leaving the place. It strikes me as odd that he should be there, but imagine that he has been visiting Goldreich or his wife in the main house. I go down the long drive to a secluded area behind the farmhouse, and park my Vauxhall next to Bernstein's car and a Combi van in which, I discover later, Denis Goldberg has brought Sisulu, Mbeki and Mhlaba from Travallyn to the meeting. Kathrada has arrived the night before. Goldberg is inside the main house.

Behind the main house there is a small thatched outhouse in which we hold our meetings. The other five are already present.

I ask whom I had seen leaving in a car. Sisulu explains that it was the dentist who was taking an impression of his mouth to enable him to improve his disguise. Kathrada says he had been much embarrassed because the dentist seemed to recognise him, despite his disguise as a Portuguese man. I am shocked that the dentist has been allowed to see others in the outhouse.

We have small items of business, which take 10 minutes to complete. I have been asked to advise the others on what is happening under the 90-day detention law, and bring with me a copy of the *Government Gazette* in which the regulations are published. Kathrada has a coded letter from Natal, which we think might relate to the mysterious visitor to my chambers that morning. Mbeki has brought with him a copy of 'Operation Mayibuye', a document I have never had a chance to read. The document is resting on Bernstein's lap because he wants to renew the objections he made at the meeting on the previous Saturday.

It is about 3.15 pm when a van is heard coming down the drive. The geese that roam between the main house and outhouses cackle loudly. Mbeki goes to the window. He says, 'It's a dry-cleaning van. I've never seen it before.' Bernstein then looks out and exclaims, 'My God, I saw that van outside the police station on the way here!' I move to the open door and see the panel of the van, which reads 'Trade Steam Pressers'. I can see a man wearing a white coat, hat and glasses in the front seat. I pull the door closed. As I do so, Thomas Mashifane, the farm manager, comes to the door with a parcel. Someone yells out, 'Go and see what that van wants.' I pull the door closed again.

The next moment I hear a dog barking. Bernstein shouts: 'It's the cops, they're heading here.' Mbeki collects the 'Operation Mayibuye' document and some other papers and I see him putting them in the small stove in the room. The back window is open, and I help Mbeki, Sisulu and Kathrada jump out of it. There is a second or two as I move back near the door, with Bernstein next to me and Mhlaba sitting next to the window. The door bursts open. D/Sgt. Kennedy, whom I cross-examined in a political trial earlier that year, rushes in: 'Stay where you are. You're all under arrest.' He walks up to me with an excited sneer: 'You're Advocate Hepple, aren't you?'

We are escorted outside and searched. Warrant Officer Dirker is already searching Sisulu, who has been caught with the others as they tried to escape. Triumphantly, he looks up and laughs at me: 'Oh Heppy, now we have you all!' This is Dirker's moment of revenge for the advice I gave Mandela during the 1962 trial to expose his improper conduct, when a prosecution witness, in escorting the magistrate for lunch.

Bernstein and I are placed in the back of a van with Mashifane and another farm worker, closely guarded by a constable and a vicious dog. After some time, I am taken back to the outhouse. Dirker shows me some ashes in an ashtray and asks, 'What did you burn here?' I reply: 'I burned nothing.' He screams, 'Don't lie.' I am then taken to my motor car. Dirker feels the bonnet to see how warm it is and searches the car. There is nothing incriminating, just as there is nothing on my person. Later I am taken to other outhouses and shown duplicating machines, paper and equipment. I say, truthfully, 'I have never seen any of these before.' Dirker asks, 'When did you come here? Who asked you to come?' I say I am not prepared to answer any questions, and he does not persist.

I am taken back to the van and painfully handcuffed to Kathrada. The uniformed constable continually provokes his fierce Alsatian dog to lunge at us, and hurls vile abuse. After about three hours, Bernstein and I are put into the enclosed laundry van. There we find Mbeki handcuffed most uncomfortably to a roof support. At this stage Goldberg is brought out of the main house, the first time I have seen him. We are joined by four policemen and driven off into the night. Mbeki manages to whisper that 'Operation Mayibuye' had been found, and says, 'This is going to be high treason, chaps.'

We arrive at the Johannesburg Fort half an hour later. This prison, known to generations of Africans as Number Four, is notorious as a place where violent criminals, pass offenders and political prisoners are held and brutally treated in disgusting conditions. The political prisoners have included Mahatma Gandhi in 1908 when leading the passive resistance movement; white labour leaders during the 1922 strike, including Hull, Lewis and Long, who were hanged; and Mandela and other Treason trialists in 1956. (Since 2003 it has been the site of the magnificent Constitutional Court.) We are all lined up. The black prisoners among us (the farm workers at Lilliesleaf were also arrested) are made to strip naked to be searched on this cold July evening, but they refuse to do the 'tausa', the ritual in which the prisoner is made to leap in the air, spinning around and opening his legs, while clapping his hands overhead and bending his body forward so as to expose the open rectum. Whites are more favourably treated than blacks. Bernstein, Goldberg and I are simply pushed into a small cell. By this time I have secreted my watch in my shoe as well as a few pencils in my socks. But this proves to be an unnecessary precaution because on this occasion we are not searched.

We agree not to talk about the raid, but soon we begin to speculate, 'Was it the dentist who revealed the place?' After 15 minutes we are separated. A convicted prisoner is moved out to make room for me. I am then alone in this and other prisons for most of the next 90 days. That night, I am too shocked and distressed to sleep, with a light shining all night in my eyes.

The next morning, four security policemen led by Lt. Kotze escort me to my chambers. A search reveals some public documents, and also a copy of a banned book Slovo had left with me. While I am there my wife and mother arrive. I am not allowed to talk to them. Although I asked the police to inform my wife of my arrest the night before, they did not do so. It was only when they read that morning's Nationalist paper *Die Transvaler* that my family discovered why I had not returned home.

Then I am taken to my home, which is searched. Nothing is discovered, and I am able to tell Shirley where I have stashed away a large sum of cash – money used to support those who are underground – and tell her to return this to Bram Fischer, who acts as the underground's treasurer. I am taken to Fordsburg police station and placed in a large, cheerless, bitterly cold cell, with a stinking open sanitary bucket in one corner. There are no windows, the walls are black and a light burns day and night. The blankets are flea-ridden and pee-stained. Suspended from the ceiling is a paper figure of a man hanging from his neck – whether this is a sick police joke or the act of a previous inmate I do not know. I spend the day pacing up and down to keep warm, thinking about our predicament. That night there is a surprise – a white prisoner is brought into my cell. I soon realise that he is probably a police spy – I say nothing much to him but he pours out his legal problems. This relieves the strain of that first day. Later that night, two drunks are thrown into the cell, and become disgustingly sick and violent.

At about 9.30 the next morning Col. Howells and Warrant Officer Nel fetch me. Later we pick up Goldberg and Bernstein. We are handcuffed, whites in one van and blacks in another, and followed by a long convoy of police cars. With us is Hilliard Festenstein, a research scientist known to everyone as 'H', who we learn was arrested when he arrived at Goldreich's house on

HOW DID THE POLICE DISCOVER LILLIESLEAF?

Fifty years after the Rivonia raid there is still speculation about how the police discovered the secret headquarters. The police gave various versions. At first, they spread a rumour that two activists, who were among the first to be detained under the 90-day law, had given the information and then been allowed to leave the country. Later, they said that Lt. Van Wyk was contacted by an informant who offered to tell him where he could find Walter Sisulu in return for a reward, reputedly R6000. Van Wyk allegedly spent a week cruising around the area with the informant, who eventually recognised the neighbourhood and a sign reading 'IVON'. This was RIVONIA with the RI and IA faded out. Van Wyk originally planned to raid the premises on the morning of 11 July, when he would have found only Kathrada there. However, Col. Venter told him to obtain a search warrant and the raid was postponed until 3 pm when he caught the whole secretariat plus Goldberg, and later the Goldreichs and Festenstein. Bruno Mtolo (Mr X), the state's star witness at the Rivonia Trial, a member of the Natal regional command of MK, was one of those who had stayed at Lilliesleaf. He gave evidence that the police drove him around until he found the place for them. But this evidence has been treated with scepticism as a police diversion from the true informant, whose identity remains unknown.

Suspicion fell on the dentist who visited the farm to take an impression of Sisulu's mouth and left at about 3 pm. The police claimed that they had the farm under surveillance for some hours before the raid at 3.15 pm, but they did not arrest

> *the dentist. I speculated that the unknown Indian man who came to my chambers on the morning of 11 July with a message might have been a police spy. Nic Wolpe and researchers at the Lilliesleaf Trust have conducted extensive inquiries and suggest that the informant may have been a radio engineer who was brought to Lilliesleaf to assess a Soviet radio transmitter that was in need of repair, or that the American CIA or British MI6 may have had information which they passed on to the South African police. Alternatively, the raid might have been triggered by information given to the police by the child of a neighbour who visited the Goldreich children, or by another neighbour whose suspicions were aroused when he came to the farm about a water problem. We are unlikely ever to know the truth, but it is obvious that many security lapses contributed to the police raid that deprived the movement of its key leaders.*

the evening of 11 July. We are being driven to Pretoria Local Prison, where the real ordeal is to begin.

Why I was there

During the raid Col. 'Tiny' Venter said to me in Afrikaans: 'I'm really surprised to find you mixed up with these dangerous communists.' I made no reply, but I had lots of time in detention to reflect on the circumstances that led to my presence on 11 July.

In November 1962, after Mandela's trial, Slovo asked me whether I was willing to receive correspondence for the 'movement' – which I understood to be the ANC or SACP – at my chambers. He said they were having difficulty in communicating because of bannings and house arrests. He thought that my address would provide a 'respectable' channel for receiving letters. I agreed to do this, and from then on I received about two letters each week postmarked from Durban or Port Elizabeth or Cape Town. The letters were addressed to me. On opening them I would usually find an inside envelope marked 'For Cedric', which I did not open. Sometimes the inside envelope was not marked. Occasionally there was no inside envelope at all, simply a letter to 'Dear Cedric' signed by 'Natalie'. I did not try to decipher the cryptic messages, usually only a series of numbers – presumably a book code, in which the sender and recipient agree on a particular book and then give each letter of the alphabet a page, line and word number. At first, I handed the letters to Slovo whose chambers were in the same building as mine. Later he asked if I would deliver them myself to Lilliesleaf Farm, which I did once or twice a week, usually on my way home or coming back from the Supreme Court in Pretoria.

One evening in April 1963, Bram Fischer came to my home. He was a short, stocky, rosy-cheeked man with an open face and steely blue eyes, still boyish-looking at the age of 55, gentle and warm in his relationships with those whom he regarded as his political 'family'. For me he was a revered father figure in the movement, a dedicated and courageous revolutionary; an Afrikaner 'aristocrat' (his grandfather was prime minister of the Orange River Colony and his father judge-president of the Orange Free State) who had sacrificed the paths of glory among his own people to make common cause with the oppressed. He belonged to a generation of communists who believed unswervingly in the Soviet Union. He once asked me if there were any writings that refuted the revelations of Stalin's crimes, so that he could show these to his daughters. When I said the evidence against Stalin was irrefutable, he shrugged his shoulders and said, 'Well, we now know what to avoid when we establish communism here.' He was a practical man whose deep convictions were not open to question, and he was impatient with theorising.

He was also a brilliant lawyer, the leading expert at the Bar on mining law and, during my period as a law lecturer at Wits before joining the Bar, I had consulted him when writing a chapter on economic and racial legislation for a book on South African law. One issue that we never thought it necessary to discuss was whether it was morally acceptable for a professional lawyer to defy laws that supported a wicked legal system. As Fischer pointed out in 1966, when the Bar Council applied to remove his name from the roll of advocates: 'Since the days of the South African War … it has been recognised that political offences, committed because of an overriding belief in the overriding moral validity of a political principle, do not in themselves justify the disbarring of a person from practising the profession of the law.' Before he was sentenced to life imprisonment he addressed the court in terms that many other lawyers engaged in struggles against totalitarian regimes would endorse: 'I accept, my Lord, the general rule that for the protection of a society laws should be obeyed. But when the laws themselves become immoral, and require the citizen to take part in an organised system of oppression – if only by his silence and apathy – then I believe that a higher duty arises. This compels one to refuse to recognise such laws.'

Fischer had recruited me during the state of emergency in 1960 to help him act as a lifeline for the underground leadership of the SACP and ANC. After I joined the Bar in January 1962, we were frequently in and out of each other's rooms on personal, political and professional matters. He and his wife Molly were also long-standing personal friends of Shirley's parents, who were active in raising funds for left-wing activities. During his visit in April 1963 he told me that the Central Committee of the SACP, of which he was chairman, had been badly depleted by house arrests and banning orders, and several members, including Slovo, Harmel and JB Marks, had been sent abroad on political missions. In the new period of repression, there was a real fear that the Central Committee itself would be wiped out. My task would be to reconstitute it. He recalled the help I had given the underground leadership in 1960. They needed me again.

I was hesitant not only for personal reasons – I had a young family and was building up a promising legal practice – but also because I believed that my cover as a Johannesburg advocate was illusory. I was well known to the security police, having been first arrested for political activity at the age of 19 in 1954, and had been an active member of the Congress of Democrats and a prominent student leader. I was working with the virtually illegal black trade unions affiliated to the South African Congress of Trade Unions, part of the Congress alliance. I had been the subject of security police raids on several occasions since 1956. I tried in the early 1960s to shield myself from police supervision. This meant keeping away from the offices of the few still-legal left-wing organisations, not openly associating with banned persons, and not taking any part in public political activities. Unfortunately, other comrades did not always respect this need for security. I had a constant stream of well-known activists to my chambers and home, requesting my help and using me as a conduit to the underground leadership. Wolpe and other attorneys were briefing me to take political cases, including that of Mandela, making me a regular opponent of the security police in open court.

There were many compromising telephone calls likely to be bugged. The most ludicrous of these took place during the heightened police activity in 1962. Slovo had someone keeping watch on The Grays, security police headquarters in Johannesburg. When this person saw sudden police activity in the middle of the night, he would phone Slovo. Slovo in turn phoned me and said, 'The Russians have landed on the moon!' I would warn others with a similarly stupid message. About half an hour after the call, in the early hours, there would be a hard knock on the door. Security police would arrive and search the house. On one such occasion, Shirley was pregnant with our second child. I told the police she could not get out of bed and they respected this. She was, in fact, lying on top of papers we did not want the police to see. They never found anything significant and had to content themselves with items such as a recording of the Red Army choir singing in Welsh!

Secret meetings, including ones attended by Mandela in 1961, and in 1962 by Harmel and Kotane, leaders of the SACP, were held in our home in Victory Park, to which Shirley and I had moved a few months after our marriage in July 1960. Slovo and his wife Ruth First lived in nearby Roosevelt Park and not infrequently dropped in for a chat or assistance. The Fischers and Eli and Violet Weinberg, all banned persons, were friends who called in to see the babies and us. Hindsight suggests that it was naïve for anyone to believe that I was the right person to act as a lifeline and also to resuscitate the movement should the leadership be taken out. I admired Fischer as a courageous man who set an example by his own dedication. I was flattered that he saw me as a protégé who could replace him if he fell in the line of duty. Slovo, another persuasive advocate, also told me that I was indispensable to the survival of the underground. So, against my better judgement, I joined the secretariat. I undertook contact work, handling large sums of money, acting as postman for internal and external correspondence, and performing a multiplicity of smaller tasks and errands for those underground. These included keeping them informed of legal developments and arrests, and discussing how to get assistance for those charged with sabotage and other offences.

Walter Sisulu

There were six of us at the meeting on 11 July. I knew three of them well: Sisulu, Kathrada and Bernstein. Sisulu, secretary-general of the ANC until the government banned him from holding political office, shared with Mandela the quality of seeing the best in everyone. Physically he was very different. He was short, stocky, light in complexion, six years older than Mandela, brought up by an illiterate family in a small peasant village in the Eastern Cape, while his mother went away to work as a domestic servant for a white family. He had only six years' primary education, unlike Mandela who had a degree and was qualified as a lawyer. At the age of 14, Sisulu left the Transkei for Johannesburg, did a variety of menial jobs before going down the mines, went to night school, started an estate agency business and joined the ANC. Mandela met him in 1941 and was impressed by his intelligence, worldly experience and fluency in English despite his lack of formal education. He became Mandela's mentor and soulmate. I first met him in 1953 when he talked to the Discussion Club, a group of left-wing whites who gathered on Friday evenings in a suburban house to debate political issues. He reported on his recent visit to the World Youth Festival in Bucharest and to the Soviet Union and China. He described what he had seen and heard in simple terms: 'China is just like one of our big townships.' He was full of admiration for the Chinese revolution of 1949, but did not hold it up as a model for South Africa. He remarked: 'There is a bit too much of Stalin in the Soviet Union.' He, like Fischer, was a supreme pragmatist, not much interested in theoretical issues.

I met him again in 1954, when my friend Sydney Shall and I hitchhiked from Johannesburg to the Eastern Cape to observe an ANC conference. There were only a few whites present. Walter quickly sought us out and gave us a warm welcome. He knew Sydney because he was one of a group of white volunteers arrested for entering a black township in Germiston without permission during the Defiance Campaign in 1952. Sisulu told me that he knew and greatly admired my father, an outspoken critic of the Nationalists in the white Parliament. He welcomed the recent formation by white supporters of the Congress of Democrats of which Sydney and I were members. He made us feel that progressive whites, particularly the youth, could make a real contribution to the struggle for democracy. He was courageous and exuded a quiet self-confidence, avoiding the limelight, and was, in Mandela's words, a 'gentle revolutionary' and 'born diplomat'.

Our paths crossed a few times in the next seven years, but it was only in 1962 that I got to know him well. He was being targeted by the security police and was arrested six times in that year. One of the charges against him was of fraud for forging his pass (the identity document and workbook that every African had to carry). He asked me to defend him. I thought the circumstantial evidence against him was quite strong. I knew – although it was not general knowledge at the time – that his father was a white magistrate who had a relationship with Walter's mother but never acknowledged him as a son. I advised him that he could avoid the pass laws by seeking re-classification as a mixed-race Coloured, a group that did not require passes. He was furious: 'I am an African and always will be an African. Please never mention my parentage to anyone.' Walter used the trial to denounce the pass laws. He was acquitted, the magistrate accepting my submission that the court should not draw an adverse inference against Sisulu simply because he was opposed to the pass laws, and that in the absence of direct evidence the circumstances did not establish guilt beyond a reasonable doubt.

More significant charges of conspiring with Mandela to incite the stay-at-home in May 1961 and furthering the aims of the ANC were brought against Sisulu two days after Mandela's arrest on 5 August 1962. The state initially intended to bring him to trial with Mandela, but then decided to separate the two cases. On 15 October he was brought to court in Johannesburg, while Mandela was in court in Pretoria. There were large demonstrations by supporters outside both courts – the government promptly banned further demonstrations. Sisulu was released on bail, but a few days later was placed by the minister under house arrest, not allowed to leave his home between 7 am and 7 pm on weekdays or after 2 pm on Saturdays until Monday morning. He could not leave the magisterial district of Johannesburg, visit any township other than Orlando West, where he lived, nor communicate with any other banned persons or receive visitors except a medical practitioner. On 4 March 1963 he was found guilty on two counts and sentenced to a total of six years' imprisonment. The magistrate refused to grant him bail pending an appeal, despite a clear and binding Supreme Court decision that in such circumstances bail had to be allowed. The only discretion the magistrate had was as to the amount of bail. Many members of the Bar were outraged when they heard what had happened. An urgent application was made to the Supreme Court the same afternoon. I was in court with Slovo. Mr Justice Galgut, a conservative but fair-minded judge, said it was not necessary to hear counsel for Sisulu and he turned his formidable guns on the prosecution for opposing bail. Sisulu was granted bail and released from prison, but a few days later he was placed under 24-hour house arrest. At this point Sisulu decided, after consulting his colleagues, that he had no option but to leave his home and family to go underground.

I saw him regularly over the next few months, when I visited Lilliesleaf Farm. He was trying to disguise himself by growing a moustache, darkening his hair and letting it grow, lightening his skin colour so as to look more like a Coloured man, and having a false dental plate fitted so as to change his facial appearance. The police were desperate to find him. His wife Albertina and son Max were detained without trial in solitary confinement and interrogated, but refused to cooperate. On 26 June, Sisulu made a defiant 15-minute broadcast from Radio Liberation, which had been set up with a transmitter at Lilliesleaf Farm: 'Sons and daughters of Africa. I speak to you from somewhere in South Africa. I have not left the country. I do not intend to leave.' The police hunt for him intensified.

Ahmed Kathrada

Ahmed Kathrada, universally known as 'Kathy', was also a long-standing comrade. He was a veteran of the Indian Congress and the Communist Party. I first met him in 1953 when I joined the Congress of Democrats, occasionally visiting his flat in Kholvad House in the busy market district of Johannesburg. He was friendly, quick-witted and perceptive and had a sharp tongue and sense of irony. He was in and out of jail for political offences for many years, and was independent-minded although fiercely loyal to the movement. In November 1962, the police were looking for him to serve yet another banning order. This did not deter him, as secretary of the Free Mandela committee, from coming to the Old Synagogue in Pretoria for the first day of Mandela's trial. Eventually the police cornered him and served the order. He was ordered back to Johannesburg and placed under house arrest. In April 1963, Slovo informed me that it had been decided that Kathy should go underground. I was sent to pick him up in Doornfontein and drive him to Lilliesleaf. There, with Goldreich's help, he was disguised as Pedro Perreira, a Portuguese man, with a reddish moustache and reddish hair. Wearing sunglasses, he was virtually unrecognisable; indeed the police did not at first know who he was when they arrested him on 11 July.

Rusty Bernstein

I had known Rusty Bernstein and his wife Hilda since I was a little boy. In the 1930s, they attended meetings of the Labour League of Youth in my parents' home in Bezuidenhout Valley. Rusty recalls in his autobiography that 'occasional meetings in their house would be interrupted by a chubby, red-cheeked little boy in pyjamas and dressing gown come to kiss his parents good night'. Rusty, a lifelong communist, was a gentle, self-effacing and unambitious man, with remarkable powers of political analysis and the capacity to express himself vividly. In 1955, volunteers from the Congress of Democrats sorted out, on the Bernsteins' living-room floor, the thousands of pieces of paper that arrived from all around the country setting out people's demands that they wanted to see in the Freedom Charter. With great skill, Rusty wove these into a document that became the rallying point and programme of the movement for the next 40 years. A series of banning orders on him meant that I did not see much of him during these years before I joined the secretariat.

Govan Mbeki and Raymond Mhlaba

Govan Mbeki had broken his house arrest in the Eastern Cape and lived at Lilliesleaf from November 1962. I had first met him at secret SACP meetings in 1960, and later had occasional encounters when I delivered mail to the farm and participated in secretariat meetings. Two years older than Sisulu, he was tall and well built, with a commanding presence. He sported a modest beard and usually wore a workman's overalls with a knitted cap pulled well down over his forehead. He was widely read, and had been a teacher, journalist and ANC organiser. I had become familiar with his writings in *New Age* and other left-wing publications in the 1950s and early 1960s, particularly on the condition of the African peasantry and their revolt against the government-imposed 'Bantu Authorities'. He was, as Colin Bundy has described him, recalling Gramsci's phrase, an 'organic intellectual', one who was not merely eloquent but an active participant in practical life, an organiser and 'permanent persuader'. At our meetings I found that, like Sisulu, Mbeki could inject the problems of common people into any discussion of tactics and strategy, putting his arguments quietly but persuasively. Unlike Sisulu, his arguments were also grounded in Marxist theory. He had a degree in economics from Unisa (South Africa's distance-learning university) and true to his Marxist convictions he regarded economic processes and class structures as the basis for politics. His analysis of white domination started from the viewpoint that the 'reserves' (later Bantustans) were reservoirs of cheap labour, in Marxist terms 'the reserve army of labour'. I discovered from our brief conversations about SACTU, in which I was involved, that he was a strong advocate of trade union organisation for urban workers. Although he shared the aspirations of Mandela and Sisulu for national liberation, he was also a dedicated communist who saw the ultimate objective as being a socialist society, and was a firm believer in the leading and independent role of the Communist Party. I noticed that in the months of his isolation at

Lilliesleaf he seemed to be becoming tougher, more militant and uncompromising, and I was to discover that he and Slovo were the key drafters of the contentious and far-fetched 'Operation Mayibuye'.

Raymond Mhlaba was the one member of the secretariat I never really got to know. A large, rather overweight man who suffered from high blood pressure (I brought him medication obtained from a friendly doctor), he was a former factory worker, a veteran communist and ANC activist from the Eastern Cape. He had recently returned from military training abroad. He usually followed Mbeki's line and said little at meetings but seemed to have a more conciliatory approach than Mbeki.

These were the men I was with in the thatched cottage when the police struck. Now we were all in detention.

Chapter Four

DETENTION WITHOUT TRIAL

13 July 1963

Solitary confinement

On arrival at Pretoria Local we are stripped naked and searched. The warder – known as 'Kaffir' du Preez because of the brutal treatment he metes out to African prisoners – seems to take particular delight in the anal probes designed to ensure that there are no concealed drugs. Goldberg is unlucky to be charged with attempting to take money and tobacco into his cell. I manage to hide a ballpoint pen in the lining of my overcoat without being seen.

I am then taken to Cell No. 3 in the white section, which is to be my solitary home. I am struck by its small size – about 10 by 8 feet – and austerity. It has a backless wooden stool and small table. In the corner there is a dirty sanitary pot. There are no other furnishings. At one end, about eight feet up, is a barred and meshed window without panes. By standing on the stool placed on the table I can see out of the window onto the small prison hospital courtyard. At the other end is a heavy steel door with a peephole which can be opened only from outside. Through a small, high, meshed opening waft the smells and noises of the prison. Every footstep or clanging door reverberates in the cell.

The grey walls are bare. The light shining through the window creates an illusion of corrugations in the high ceiling. At night, I lie awake trying to count them.

There is a neatly rolled pile of smelly blankets but no bed or mattress, so one sleeps on the cold black floor, without a pillow. At midday a small ray of sunlight enters my north-facing cell. I wait anxiously each day for the warm solace of the sun on my face. As winter passes into spring this daily quotient of sun disappears altogether. I am not allowed a watch and the warders will not tell me the time. So I make a sun-clock with tiny pencil marks on the walls.

I get hold of this pencil in a rather curious way. White prisoners awaiting trial clean the corridors. One day, as the corridors (which I cannot see) are being cleaned, a tiny pencil suddenly appears in the small opening, accessible only from the corridor, in which a light bulb is encased. With the aid of a spoon and thread I manage to extricate the pencil – I never discover who my benefactor is.

The only other way of keeping track of the time is by the regular meals. At 5.30 each morning a waking bell is sounded in the courtyard. Half an hour later Head Warder Breedt opens the door and shouts '*Alles* (Everything) all right, Hepple?' and closes it again without waiting for a reply. A few minutes later the door is opened again. A tin bowl of mealie (maize) meal porridge, usually already cold, has been placed next to the door. I have to grab it quickly in one hand, while a mug of black coffee is thrust into the other. Then the door is slammed shut again.

I then busy myself cleaning the cell, with the rags and lump of polish supplied. An hour waltzing around on the rags produces one of those ultra-shiny floors of which polish manufacturers would be proud. Blankets have to be precisely folded according to prison rules. 'Kaffir' du Preez finds it amusing to pull mine apart and make me start all over again. Between 10 am and noon there is an inspection by the prison commandant, Colonel Aucamp. This is a farcical routine. One has to stand to stiff attention at the door, while he walks briskly past. No word is exchanged, although this is supposed to be an opportunity for prisoners to voice their grievances. Lunch is thrust through the door, often cold, at 11.30. The long prison 'nights' start between 3 and 4 pm after a plate of thick soup, a slice of brown bread and a mug of coffee. Shoes (no laces are allowed) are placed outside the door, and one is locked in until the next morning.

I follow the cleaning routine each morning by walking 300 to 400 times up and down the cell. I walk again in the afternoon and evening, doing several miles a day in this confined space. As I pace up and down my thoughts are on my family, my comrades, and how we got into this mess. Without realising it, as the endless days go on I wander increasingly into realms of fantasy and superstition. I find myself creating associations of numbers – such as, today is the 29th, 9 plus 2 is 11, so 11 is a lucky number.

Some time after 8.30 am, the four white 'politicals' – Bernstein, Goldberg, Festenstein and I – are taken out together into the prison yard. We have half an hour to shave in cold water, take a cold shower, and clean out our water bowls and sanitary buckets. The yard is surrounded by high prison walls, and above is what Oscar Wilde in 'The Ballad of Reading Gaol' described as 'the small tent of blue that prisoners call the sky'. In winter the yard catches only a hint of sunshine, but by spring it is warm and sunny. In the middle of the yard is an open block of two toilets, two showers and a urinal. At first I spend as much time as possible energetically jogging around the yard. As my mental state deteriorates I become languid, walk around a few times but am mostly slumped against the wall.

We are closely supervised during these half-hour breaks by two to four warders. We are not permitted to communicate in any way, but we soon find ways to pass each other notes. With a good supply of toilet paper and a smuggled pen or pencil one can compose a message in minute script and find a way to leave it in the toilet for the next user to pick up. Bernstein and I manage to maintain a dialogue for some weeks. He has a gift with words, and keeps up my spirits with his Gilbert and Sullivan parody – the prison commandant is 'the very model of a model major-general'. This and other notes, with advice or comfort to each other, are written either on toilet paper or on the backs of chocolate paper – our families are allowed to send in small comforts like chocolate and fruit.

Another thread of life comes from awaiting-trial prisoners who sometimes leave a newspaper concealed in the toilets. Each of us takes a turn on the seat, with eyes seriously fixed to the ground as if having a difficult motion, avidly reading a week-old paper. This is soon discovered, and all newspapers are carefully removed before the politicals enter the yard. The awaiting-trial prisoners are always cleared away when we have to walk along the corridors.

The passing of notes comes to an end after a few weeks. We are joined by a surprise prisoner, Jimmy Kantor, whom I know as an attorney and brother-in-law and partner in the legal practice of Harold Wolpe. Kantor is usually a cheerful, happy-go-lucky man, a socialite and completely non-political. He has no connection with Lilliesleaf or the underground. Bernstein passes him a note, asking why he has been detained. Kantor replies in a message passed on to me that Wolpe was arrested a few days after the Rivonia raid, while trying to flee the country, but had managed to escape with Goldreich from Marshall Square police station by offering a bribe to a policeman. A manhunt for them is going on and Kantor has been detained by way of retaliation, in effect as a hostage. With no experience of underground work, Kantor files Bernstein's note neatly in his Bible. It is discovered when he is being removed to Johannesburg. The security men swoop into the prison and interrogate each of us as to whether we have any contact. That evening I am removed from Cell No. 3 into the smaller Cell No. 9, away from sight or sound of my colleagues. On the wall is an inscription by David Pratt, a well-to-do white farmer who had attempted to assassinate Prime Minister Verwoerd in 1960 and later killed himself in this prison. The warder pointedly gives me the creeps by demonstrating how Pratt strangled himself with a blanket tied to the window bars in this very cell, almost inviting me to do the same.

The next morning we have a longer-than-usual exercise period. When I return to my cell it is a shambles. Every blanket lining has been ripped open, the toilet roll unravelled, clothes pulled apart – as if there has been a tornado. As I start gathering up my belongings, I notice that all my carefully collected pencil stubs have gone. A diary which I have been secretly keeping, by then for about 48 days, and had hidden in my overcoat lining was missing, and some letters I had written on toilet tissues, hidden at the bottom of a box, are also gone. Even a piece of paper on which I had drawn a draughts board has been confiscated.

That is the end of all communication between the four of us. We are rigidly kept apart and regimented from then on, and are closely watched in the yard. We have to use the toilets separately, and after each person the warders make a search. On entering and leaving the yard we are stripped and body-searched. The yard is divided into four 'quarters' and we each have to remain in our own quarter. There are sporadic snap cell raids, in which blankets, clothes and possessions are thrown about. On entering the cell the warder screams at me for *slordigheid* (untidiness), and threatens to deprive me of food or exercise breaks. This humiliating treatment continues for weeks.

After my writing paper is confiscated, I still have a hidden pen and resort to writing on toilet paper and chocolate wrappings. But the warders begin to unwrap every sweet, chocolate and other wrapping that comes with food parcels from the outside. The use of toilet paper is all that remains, and since this is rationed I not infrequently find myself high and dry on the toilet. We find a way in which to smuggle in writing instruments – in the bananas sent with our food parcels. This leads to rather difficult moments for Bernstein, who cannot eat bananas himself, and one day, having forgotten the possibility of ballpoint pen refills being inside the banana, gives it away to an awaiting-trial prisoner. Fortunately the warders do not discover it, but they must have their suspicions because from time to time they break open fruit, butter and other soft foods sent in to us. Bernstein is a man of great ingenuity, and discovers that he can smuggle notes in the collars of his washing, which is collected each week by our wives. We get occasional snatches of news this way, which proves tremendously heartening.

There is no reading matter. I know that prison regulations allow every prisoner a Bible. I demand one, and after four days the King James Bible, which I have possessed since childhood but rarely read since I was at school, arrives, sent in by my family. It proves to be a lifesaver. During my time in solitary I read both the Old and New Testament twice, and learn many of the psalms by heart. I find it difficult to concentrate, but my daily quota of reading the Bible helps to keep me going. It takes my mind into another realm, and I discover the solace of prayer. On the back cover I make a list of the biblical generations, and also draw a draughts board, using spit balls of toilet paper as the pieces. I play 'cricket', rolling a pencil with numbers on its sides along the table and record the 'scores'. After a raid on our cells, the pencil is removed and the games have to stop.

As the prison quietens each evening, singing begins – the harmonious but distant voices from the African section weakly matched by the white politicals. The warders rush about wildly trying to stop it, but even a few refrains are soothing and inspiring.

I do not sleep for more than four hours a night, and then only lightly. More than once a warder bursts into the cell while I am dozing, saying that I screamed out. With so many anxieties and awful nightmares, this is not surprising. In the long hours of isolation and boredom, especially as I lie on the hard, cold stone floor, I become obsessed with my predicament and can think of little else. As the days and nights slowly pass, I become increasingly confused and create my own world in which reality and fantasy are hard to separate. I worry about small things – such as where a particular sound in the prison is coming from – a gong, a scream, a clanging gate.

I worry especially about the letters on toilet paper that were confiscated. I was highly emotional when I wrote them, and I cannot remember their content: had I revealed anything or disclosed our means of communication with the outside world? I know that I insulted the warders in my diary – one in particular as a 'little fascist shit' – and after its discovery, they retaliate by daily stripping and searching, tripping me up in the corridor, leaving my food outside my door until it is cold, and countless other humiliations.

These experiences as a white detainee are as nothing compared to the inhuman treatment of African prisoners. I witness the horrifying effects of detention on Zeph Mothopeng, a PAC detainee. One night in September, I am woken by screams emanating from the African section. These continue all night. The next morning I hear a screaming man being pushed along the corridor into the hospital yard. I stand on the stool, which I have placed on my table, and there see that it is Mothopeng being held by two warders with arms twisted behind his back. He is foaming at the mouth and his eyes have the wide, vacant stare of the berserk. A few days later I see him in the yard again, in a straitjacket, his screams by then whimpers, each of which is met by a blow from the warders. (Mothopeng sued the government for damages but he was unsuccessful. Instead he was jailed for PAC activities.)

Legalised torture

My initial reaction to detention was legalistic. I wrote a letter dated 18 July, a week after the arrests, to Vorster, the minister of justice. I had examined the '90-day' law closely before my arrest in order to advise the families of detainees. The notorious section 17 of the General Law Amendment Act No. 37 of 1963 (the Sabotage Act) allowed a commissioned officer to arrest 'any person whom he suspects upon reasonable grounds of having committed or intending to commit' sabotage or an offence relating to banned political organisations, such as the ANC and SACP. The police officer could also arrest anyone 'who in his opinion is in possession of information' relating to these offences. In the first six months (May to November 1963) 544 persons were detained under the 90-day law. In the whole of 1963 another 2811 were detained under other repressive laws. Detention without trial in any country gives the executive and police powers that Winston Churchill described as being 'in the highest degree odious'. It not only deprives a person of the judgment of an independent court, but it is also usually cloaked in secrecy; as such, it is incompatible with the rule of law.

The South African version was no exception to this and went even further. It was the brainchild of the minister of justice, Balthazar Johannes Vorster, known as 'John', born in 1915, the thirteenth son of an Afrikaner farmer. He studied law at Stellenbosch University, where he came under the influence of Verwoerd. In 1940 he joined the militant, anti-democratic, national-socialist Ossewa-Brandwag, which supported Hitler. He was arrested on suspicion of high treason, and detained without trial, so he was well versed in methods of suppressing opposition. Verwoerd made him minister of justice in 1961. He immediately embarked on an intensive campaign against the extra-parliamentary opposition. He quadrupled the security police force and brought in numerous laws aimed at crushing the Congress alliance and other political movements campaigning for an end to white domination. He banned hundreds from political, trade union and journalistic work, and placed some under 12-hour or 24-hour house arrest. The 'cruellest and most effective instrument of modern torture' he invented to break the resistance movement was the 90-day law. In 1998, the Truth and Reconciliation Commission (TRC) concluded that the 90-day law marked the beginning of the systematic use of torture by the security police, both as a means of obtaining information and of terrorising activists.

Detainees had no access to legal advisers or any other person without police permission. Vorster sought to justify the removal of the basic human right to see a lawyer by asserting that those arrested for political reasons 'always ask to see the same lawyer', and he named six well-known left-wing attorneys and advocates whom he regarded as 'undesirable'. There were, of course, eminent lawyers with no particular sympathy for the cause of the accused in political cases who ably defended them and ensured their acquittal. However, there was a fear among the legal profession that any lawyer who represented a political detainee would be dubbed a 'subversive', so they found reasons for declining to act – despite the so-called taxi-rank rule that obliges a lawyer to accept a brief, however unpopular the cause. The real reason for denying access to lawyers was that they were regarded as a 'nuisance' to police who were trying to obtain a confession or information. Lawyers are usually able to ensure that no force, threat or promise is used in obtaining statements. This was an obstacle to the police that the Sabotage Act removed. It soon emerged that detainees were being subjected to physical torture, including electric shocks and waterboarding. Many detainees were forced to make statements and were either charged or became state witnesses. In 1963 five 90-day detainees had to be referred to psychiatrists, and one (Looksmart Khulile Ngudle) became the first of many to die in detention after being tortured. Babla Saloojee, who helped us and many others to escape, was arrested on 6 July 1964 and died in police custody on 9 September 1964. It is now generally accepted that he was severely tortured, killed and thrown out of the seventh floor of The Grays, the security police building, although an inquest found that he had 'committed suicide'.

Unlike earlier 'preventive' detention, which was imposed during wartime and in the 1960 state of emergency in order to take suspected subversives out of circulation, the express and sole purpose of detaining persons under the 90-day law was for interrogation, by methods that would induce them to speak. Solitary confinement, the withdrawal of reading and writing materials, and deprivation of human contact were part of the process of 'softening up'. When introducing the legislation, Vorster said that its purpose was 'to ferret out the leaders of the subversive movement responsible for acts of sabotage'. He made it quite clear that it was intended to put psychological and physical pressure on detainees so that they would give the police information.

The person could be detained at 'any place' the police 'think fit'. Many detainees were made to stand like a statue for hours in a chalk circle in front of the police officers. Norman Levy has recounted how in 1964 he was made to stand in this way for 102 hours while being interrogated. When detainees complained, they were told that the chalk circle was a 'place' and the Act did not prescribe any limits on its size or location. There was no way this could be challenged in court – unless the detainee could smuggle out a message – because detainees were not allowed access to a lawyer, doctor or any other outside person without police permission.

The only exception was a weekly visit from a magistrate. Those visits were a formality. The magistrate noted my complaints. When I asked the magistrate, 'What will happen to my complaint?', he simply wrote down 'What will happen to my complaint?' No action resulted. On one such occasion I saw an African comrade, Andrew Mlangeni (later one of the Rivonia accused sentenced to life imprisonment), in the corridor waiting for the magistrate. He whispered to me that he had been tortured, and showed me the burn marks from the infliction of electric shocks. The following year, when a detainee, Ivan Schermbrucker, managed to smuggle out a note that he was being subjected to cruel and inhuman interrogation, the courts decided that the Act debarred them from ordering the production of a detainee. In the Roman-Dutch common law of South Africa, a court could normally order the production of a person being detained or mistreated in custody through an interdict *de homine libero exhibendo* (the equivalent of the English common law writ of *habeas corpus*) but this remedy was denied to 90-day detainees. The detention could last until such time as 'in the opinion of the Commissioner' the detainee had 'replied satisfactorily to all questions' at the interrogation. The maximum period at first was 90 days 'on any particular occasion' a person was arrested. The police soon started to re-arrest detainees immediately at the end of 90 days, a practice upheld as lawful by the courts. When lawyers acting for Albie Sachs later sought to challenge the right of the authorities to deprive a detainee of all reading and writing materials, the highest court ruled that this form of psychological pressure was permitted by the statute because its purpose was to induce the detainee to speak. The supine attitude of the courts to this legislation was one of the most disgraceful and revealing features of the police state.

The 90-day law in effect permitted legalised torture. It was followed in 1965 by 180-day detention without trial, and in 1967 by indefinite detention. One of the great achievements of the European Enlightenment of the 18th century was the ending of judicially sanctioned torture. The infliction of physical pain and degradation in order to extract confessions and the names of accomplices and, at the same time, to instil terror in the populace of the power of the state, had long been part of the legal process. Until the mid-17th century, the Star Chamber in England arrested and imprisoned people on the slightest suspicion, and it issued orders to justices of the peace, who interrogated suspects under torture. Courageous men like John Lilburne, who refused to be interrogated, were whipped and pilloried. This was incompatible with the claims by Enlightenment thinkers such as Thomas Hobbes, of the right to life and to the integrity of one's body.

By the early years of the 19th century, English criminal procedure, which was incorporated into legal practice in the British colonies in South Africa, had taken away the power of magistrates to interrogate an accused person. It was also accepted that 'third degree' methods should not be allowed and that no person should be obliged to answer questions that would incriminate him or her. This last privilege – against self-incrimination – was the most important of all. It became a fundamental principle of justice throughout the Anglo-Saxon world and part of the law of South Africa. In fact, the first Criminal Code of the Union of South Africa passed in 1917 went even further. Besides the privilege against self-incrimination, confessions made to the police were rendered inadmissible in evidence unless confirmed and reduced to writing before a magistrate. Moreover, there were rules formulated by the judges, which were issued as administrative directions to the police, to protect suspects from self-incrimination. But in the case of political suspects, the Sabotage Act swept aside these provisions. Ninety-day detainees lost all the traditional privileges of suspects and witnesses: they could be required to answer incriminating questions, they could be compelled to give evidence against their own spouse, professional advisers could be asked to inform the police what their clients had communicated to them, and confessions made to the police, without the intervention of a magistrate, became admissible. Those confessions still had to be made freely and voluntarily, but the courts ruled that a confession made by a 90-day detainee in solitary confinement was admissible because the statutory obligation to answer questions removed the privilege against self-incrimination.

The South African laws authorising detention without trial prevented victims of torture from gaining access to the courts to complain about their treatment. Their most devastating effect came through psychological torture by permitting isolation and interrogation without restraint. The South African Criminal

Code had previously restricted the use of solitary confinement (as a punishment for offences in prison) to no more than two days a week. Now it was used continuously for indefinite periods. The use of psychological conditioning to induce people to make confessions was not new. It was in Stalin's Russia that these techniques were most wickedly refined, leading lifelong communists to confess to treachery and sabotage. Ironically, the South African police, the declared enemies of communism, had no qualms about emulating the communist police states in this respect. The TRC found that a number of security police officers, including Hendrik van den Bergh (head of the Security Branch) and TJ ('Rooi Rus') Swanepoel, received training in torture techniques in France and Algeria in the early 1960s. The essential aim of these techniques is to induce feelings of anxiety, mental conflict and guilt, and to impair the normal functioning of the brain. In his classic study, *Battle for the Mind*, William Sargant shows that without physical violence one or more physiological methods can be used to induce apparently 'voluntary' confessions. These methods include deliberately stirring up anxiety, prolonging tension to a point when the brain becomes exhausted and inhibited, bombarding the brain with a variety of stimuli in the form of ever-changing attitudes and questions by the examiners so that the subject becomes confused, and taking additional measures such as sleep deprivation to finally cause a breakdown of brain function and resistance.

The limits of law
At the time of my arrest the 90-day law had been in operation for only two months. One of the great weaknesses of the Congress movement was that we had not prepared ourselves to resist these new techniques of torture. Nor had we faced up to the likelihood that detainees would break and reveal

information about themselves and others. The standard advice to anyone arrested by the security police was 'Refuse to answer any questions'. Some detainees doggedly and bravely managed to do so. But, as Sargant says, 'granted the right pressure is applied in the right way and for long enough, ordinary prisoners have little chance of staving off collapse; only the exceptional or mentally ill person is likely to resist over very long periods'. We ignored the fact that the security police had now taken off the kid gloves and were willing to use subtle forms of psychological torture as well as brutal physical methods.

The letter I wrote to the minister of justice just a week after my arrest aimed, rather naïvely, to put the legal limits of the new law to the test. I said:

(a) since my arrest on 11 July until today, i.e. a period of 7 days, I have not been interrogated;

(b) since my arrest I have been lodged in a cell on my own and I have not been allowed any communication whatsoever with any other detainee and/or awaiting trial prisoner;

(c) since my arrest I have not been allowed any reading matter other than the Bible (which I received on the fourth day of my detention) nor have I been permitted to engage in any other kind of recreative activity (save for normal prison exercise periods);

(d) since my arrest the only visit I have been allowed was one of five minutes' duration by my wife ... which was entirely inadequate to discuss family and professional matters requiring my attention, with her.

I went on to ask him to direct that I be released, subject to remaining available for interrogation at such time and place as the police might ask, to allow me the company of other persons and reading and writing materials so long as I remained in detention, and to allow further visits by my wife. A week later I wrote to the commissioner of police saying that I had still not been interrogated, and that this had led me to the conclusion 'that my detention is not bona fide for the purposes of interrogation'. I also drafted a petition to the court submitting that my detention was unreasonable and for an ulterior purpose, and seeking an order that I be produced in court and that the minister and police show cause why I should not be released. I learned later that these documents had not been sent to the minister or the court. Rather, they were in the hands of the security police.

The legal approach proved to be futile. Worse, it put me in the false position of asking to be interrogated, when the last thing I wanted to do was to give the police information. I hoped that they would believe me if I told them that I was at Lilliesleaf to give the outlaws legal advice. But perhaps subconsciously I was craving human contact and conversation, and deluding myself about the possibility of an early release. I was relying on my intelligence and critical powers to ensure that I made only harmless statements of indisputable facts to the police. What I did not recognise is that during the weeks of being held in solitary confinement with no recourse to the outside world, my power to reason was being corrupted. The police and warders were piling up the psychological pressure, prolonging the tension, so that, even before my interrogation started, my thinking was being distorted. My anxiety reached its climax when Lt. Van Wyk unexpectedly visited me in my cell on 25 July with some news that delighted him but shocked me.

Chapter Five

'YOU WILL ALL BE HANGED'
25 July 1963

The shock

Two weeks in detention have passed. I am sitting in my cell drafting my petition to the Pretoria Supreme Court. I hear the familiar footsteps of the warder, the clanging of gates and jangling of keys. I see an eye peering through the peephole in my solid cell door. The door is noisily opened. In walks Lt. Willem Petrus van Wyk, who led the raid on Lilliesleaf Farm, a short dapper man with thick eyebrows, dark wavy hair, a neat moustache and a large, apparently friendly smile on his face. Behind him is Detective Warrant Officer Dirker with the same wide turned-down hat covering the upper part of his face that he was wearing when we were arrested. He is a broad, tall, overweight man, with a flushed round face, an upturned V-shaped moustache, balding hair and a grim expression. He towers menacingly behind Van Wyk. He knows me well from Mandela's 1962 trial and other political cases in which I have cross-examined him. He has a reputation for nastiness. I am aware of the contrast between the two men – one a young, intelligent, friendly smooth talker; the other a much older man, thuggish, threatening and dim-witted (he repeatedly failed the examination to become a lieutenant). The warder locks the door behind them and waits outside.

I stand up. Van Wyk is polite. He greets me by asking, 'Everything okay?' Dirker glowers. Van Wyk says that the police have the letter I wrote to the minister, and that they are very busy investigating my involvement. They have the evidence of witnesses that I had visited Lilliesleaf before 11 July. I realise that by now Thomas Mashifane, the farm manager, and other farm workers must have been interrogated, possibly tortured, and could have identified me. (In the subsequent Rivonia trial Mashifane testified that, in solitary confinement, he had been made to take off all his clothes and was then beaten and kicked as he ran naked around a table.) 'Tell us what you were discussing,' Van Wyk says. I know that they have found a copy of the 'Operation Mayibuye' document in the thatched cottage where we were meeting, but I do not reply to his question. Then he gives me a piece of information that comes as a tremendous shock.

'We took away cartloads of documents at Lilliesleaf. Lists of addresses, records of the ANC, a firearm and explosives.' He adds, almost as an afterthought: 'We even found Mandela's diaries and scores of other documents in his handwriting. The diaries give details of all his meetings when he visited African states. The notes set out the plans for his escape last year when you were defending him. There are notes about guerrilla warfare and revolution, and a big writing pad about communism.'

I can scarcely believe this. I have never seen the diaries and notes but I had passed on a message from Mandela the previous November during his trial that all his documents should be removed or destroyed. Sisulu brought a similar message after he met Mandela in prison shortly after Mandela's arrest in August 1962, as did Slovo. Responsibility for keeping Lilliesleaf clear of documents rested with those living there, and this had apparently been delegated to Goldreich. I find out later

91

that instead of disposing of Mandela's papers as instructed, Goldreich had buried them in a box beneath the coalshed next to the kitchen of the main house in the belief that these 'historical' documents should be preserved. Mbeki, who was staying there from November 1962, was repeatedly told to ensure that everything was removed. On the Saturday before the raid, when we were arranging the meeting for 11 July, Mbeki assured us that Lilliesleaf was clean. Judging from Mbeki's reaction after the arrests, I believe that he genuinely thought that Goldreich had cleared up. He had obviously failed to do so. I realise that, as a result, Mandela will now be put on trial for his life.

Van Wyk senses my shock. He rubs it in: 'Those documents and Operation Mayibuye mean that Mandela and the rest of you will be sentenced to death for treason and sabotage.' I know that the common law offence of treason carries the death penalty. The prosecution had found that offence too difficult to prove in the long-running Treason Trial, but if it could now be shown that the accused were planning the use of sabotage to overthrow the white state, that would be treasonable. I also know that the Sabotage Act of 1962 has created a new offence of sabotage, with a minimum five-year sentence and a maximum penalty of death. This statutory offence is far easier to prove than common law treason. In a charge of treason every overt act has to be proved by two witnesses; in sabotage only a single witness is required. Moreover, the presumption of innocence is reversed. When sabotage is charged, the defendant has to prove that the commission of the act 'objectively regarded' is not calculated or intended to produce certain effects. These effects include bringing about any social or economic change in the country. In treason cases it is necessary to hold a preliminary examination, which enables the defendants to know the nature and strength of the case against them. There is no preliminary examination in a sabotage trial.

I know enough about the legal doctrine of common purpose to realise that, despite the fact that I have never been a member of MK or planned or participated in an act of sabotage, I can fairly easily be linked to the conspiracy. I have been carrying secret messages to and from those planning the acts of sabotage. Although I do not know the details of their plans, I am likely to be held to be part of their common purpose. At this point Dirker speaks out. He plays the hard man: 'We know that you hid "Operation Mayibuye" in the chimney. You were part of this.' This is not true. However, I know Dirker well enough – from other political trials and by his reputation – to fear that he will 'plant' such evidence on me. Van Wyk plays the soft man: 'Just tell us what you were discussing and why you were there, and we'll guarantee an indemnity.' He adds that they would then call me as a state witness. I reply, 'I'll never do that.' As they leave my cell, Van Wyk notices the writing pad and pen. 'Enjoy yourself with those,' he says slyly. The next day the head warder takes them away, no doubt on Van Wyk's instructions. They are piling on the pressure.

Another policeman visits me, demanding my fingerprints. I protest that since I have not been charged with any offence he has no power to take fingerprints. I argue legalistically that 'detention' for interrogation is not the same as an 'arrest' on specific charges, which the law requires before fingerprints can be taken without consent. He responds that I am going to be charged the next day with membership of a banned organisation. I am relieved because this will mean the end of 90-day detention and it suggests that they are not going to press sabotage charges against me. My resolve weakened, I let him take the fingerprints 'under protest'. But what he says is simply a ruse. The following days come and go but there are no charges.

On 30 July D/Sgt. Kennedy, who had arrested me at

Lilliesleaf, calls me out of my cell to the interrogation room in the prison. He is accompanied by another officer, whom I have never met before. He is the round-faced, bull-necked Lt. Theunis Jacobus Swanepoel. As mentioned, he is known as *Rooi Rus* (Red Russian), possibly a corruption of *rooi roes* (brown rust) because of the reddish colour of his crew-cut hair and his ruddy complexion. He has the build of an immovable rugby lock forward, small, fierce eyes, and an intimidating, angry and impatient look about him. (Swanepoel was one of the chief security police interrogators for 12 years from 1963. He became notorious as one detainee after another complained about the brutal and sadistic treatment they received from him. One of these, Mac Maharaj, later minister of transport in the Mandela government, described how he was tortured by Swanepoel in 1964 by having his penis beaten with a stick studded with rusty nails and was hung by his ankles from a seventh-floor window, the same way in which it is believed Swanepoel murdered Babla Saloojee. Swanepoel was promoted to captain and later major, and achieved further notoriety as the officer who gave the order to fire at the protesting schoolchildren of Soweto in 1976. He died quietly in retirement on his pension, still paid by the Mandela government, in 1998. He never claimed amnesty from the TRC, and was never put on trial.)

Our meeting is brief. 'What do you have to tell us?' asks Kennedy. I say, 'Nothing. Why have I not been charged as your colleague said I would be?' They laugh. I say, 'I'll petition the court for the confiscation of the illegally obtained fingerprints.' They laugh again and say that no petition will ever reach the court. They ask a second time for a statement. I decline. They call the warder to take me back to my cell. Their parting words are: 'Don't call us, we'll call you.'

On 2 August Swanepoel returns, with Warrant Officer Nel.

They say that if I give a 'reasonable' explanation of why I went to Lilliesleaf, I will be immediately released. They seem friendly and give me the impression that they mean what they say. All I have to do is to provide an innocent explanation of my presence and I will be free. By then I have been detained in solitary for three weeks. I don't recognise how much my judgement is impaired. I am emotionally and physically exhausted. I tell them to return after the weekend when I will give my reply. I now have to think seriously about making a statement, in the hope that it will secure my release. I lie awake all night wrapped in blankets on the cold stone floor of my prison cell. I have many secrets to conceal, in particular about the moves towards armed struggle and my involvement since 1960 in the underground SACP.

Moving towards armed struggle

As it sinks in that the police have been handed on a plate all the evidence they need to secure convictions for treason or sabotage, I reflect on my involvement in the SACP and the arguments within the liberation movement over the past decade about armed struggle. Mandela had been arguing for a long time that peaceful methods had been tried and failed, and that an armed struggle was inevitable. I heard him say this in the speech in Sophiatown in 1953 that earned him a rebuke from the ANC leadership. In the same year, at Mandela's instigation, Sisulu met Chinese leaders in Beijing and told them about the possibility of armed struggle. He asked whether they would supply arms. The Chinese had urged caution and said that the ANC should analyse the objective situation very carefully before reaching a decision.

By the late 1950s violent resistance had erupted in the rural areas. The government had begun to introduce 'grand' apartheid, to entrench the racial division of South Africa, allocating

95

only 13 per cent of the land to 70 per cent of the population. The so-called Bantustans (formerly 'native reserves') would be nominally independent, but two-thirds of Africans lived in white areas and they could have citizenship only in these Bantustans. There was fierce, often violent resistance to the imposition of Bantu Authorities in Eastern Pondoland, Thembuland, Zululand and Sekhukhuneland. Women in rural areas who were holding mass demonstrations against the pass laws, which were being extended to them, met with police violence.

I was able to get a small glimpse of the way in which the uprisings were being repressed. Shulamith Muller, a courageous attorney who was acting for the Bafurutse people after their chief had been deposed, briefed me to go to Sekhukhuneland – a journey of about 320 kilometres from Johannesburg – to defend a man who had resisted the police and was now charged with assault and obstruction. I took with me the legendary ANC organiser and Treason trialist Gert Sibande – known as the 'Lion of the East' – who was in touch with the peasant organisations. The night before the court hearing he took me to a clandestine gathering in a peasant hut of men and women who described to me how their homes had been burned down, they had been beaten and their leaders deported or imprisoned. Sibande, who faced arrest if he was found in the area, melted away among the people when I made my way to the remote native commissioner's court.

On arrival, I was first challenged for being in a 'Bantu' area without permission, and then told that the accused man had been taken to another village and the case would be postponed. No one would tell me where he was. When I told the commissioner, who insisted on being addressed in Afrikaans, in no uncertain terms that it was his duty to require the police to produce the man in court and that if he did not do so I was going straight to the Supreme Court, he became angry and threatened me with contempt of court proceedings. I sat down and refused to leave the court. After several hours, in which I was not offered even a glass of water, the man arrived, handcuffed, exhausted, bruised and in a frightful condition. He told me that he had been beaten up and kept without food in a filthy shed for several days while the police tried to extract a confession. After I had demanded his production, he was made to run several miles to the commissioner's court. I applied for his immediate release, but the commissioner announced that he would postpone the hearing for a week, which meant I would have to return and the man would stay in prison. A few days later I received a telephone call to say that all charges were being withdrawn and the man had been released. There were many other rural activists who were not so fortunate.

When he gave evidence in the fourth year of the Treason Trial in 1960, Mandela voiced the then policy of the ANC that in trying to persuade the white population to embrace democracy and the programme of the Freedom Charter, it would not retaliate with violence against the violence and armed force of the government. But during the 1960 state of emergency he and his fellow Treason trialists were in fact discussing not whether there should be a change to this non-violent strategy, but how and when it should occur. We were all aware that the Sharpeville massacre of 21 March 1960 – when the police opened fire on an unarmed crowd of protesters against the pass laws, killing 69 people and wounding 178, many of them shot in the back while running away – was a turning point. The subsequent state of emergency and the outlawing of the ANC and PAC created the mood among all sections of the African opposition for armed resistance. The African Resistance Movement (ARM), composed largely of disaffected members of the Liberal Party and anti-SACP Trotskyites, launched a sabotage campaign in October 1961. The PAC decided to do so in September 1961 and launched the Azanian People's Liberation Army (APLA). The emergence of the SACP and decisions taken at its conference in December 1960 were crucial to the decision by the ANC in 1961 to launch an armed struggle.

Collapse of the SACP during the state of emergency

At the critical moment on 29 March 1960, when Africans started a three-day stay-at-home and responded to a call by the ANC to burn their passes, the ANC and SACP were totally unprepared for the predictable state repression that followed. For a brief time, the government panicked and suspended the pass laws, but then on 30 March declared a state of emergency, detained without trial more than 2000 activists, and (10 years after the SACP had been banned) declared the ANC and PAC illegal organisations. Some leaders fled to neighbouring British Protectorates or went to Europe. The ANC and SACP had been unable to take advantage of a potentially revolutionary situation because of their lack of an effective underground network and basic organisational weaknesses.

I later learned that the arrests and departures in March and April 1960 had deprived the SACP of well over half its membership. In Johannesburg the entire district committee of eight or nine people was arrested in the first wave; in the next, members of a second-level replacement district committee were either arrested or fled the country. Two members of the Central Committee (Kotane and Harmel) managed to avoid arrest by going underground as a result of a chance 'tip-off'. They remained in hiding throughout the emergency. Another surviving member of the Central Committee, Bram Fischer, was not arrested. In addition, Ben Turok had escaped arrest and at an early stage established contact with the remaining Central Committee members. They formed themselves into a new centre. They had difficulty in establishing contact with surviving members, in part because a secret list of contacts was 'lost' by Harmel. I can remember Fischer, usually a calm man but highly conscious of the need for security, losing his temper, going red in the face and shouting at Harmel because of this sloppiness. Despite these difficulties, the new centre set about rebuilding the Party organisation in Johannesburg by putting together a list of people who they knew or believed had been in the Party before but had not been arrested or fled. This enabled them to set up a third-tier district committee in Johannesburg. My first contact with the rump Central Committee occurred around the end of April 1960.

Just before the emergency was declared, the National Executive Committee (NEC) of SACTU had appointed me with absolute powers to 'keep SACTU alive' should the NEC be arrested in the expected emergency – in the words of the organisation's historians, 'a gigantic task'. In this regard SACTU seems to have taken more precautions than the Party. The expected happened and I immediately set about this task. I established contact with Don Mateman, Lawrence Ndzanga and Uriah Maleka, the only active SACTU management committee members still in the country. We formed a provisional NEC of SACTU, which met almost daily and gradually re-established contacts with the workers' groups. I took personal responsibility for maintaining the Laundry Workers' Union (every one of its senior officials had been arrested) and the Metal Workers' Union, whose secretary, Gilbert Hlalukana, had fled (eventually making his way to East Germany) to avoid arrest. I was, at the time, a law lecturer at Wits. It was unsafe to work from SACTU offices, where Shanti Naidoo and Rita Ndzanga took charge, and I operated mainly from the law offices of Shulamith Muller (who had been detained). I had the help of her assistant Shirley Goldsmith, whom I married in July 1960. I worked closely with Shirley, a dedicated and loyal member of SACOD, visiting exiled SACTU officials in Swaziland and Basutoland in order to consult them on important organisational and administrative matters. The reception room in Shirley's office was full of trade unionists each day, waiting to see me about their legal and financial problems as they struggled to keep their organisations alive. I no longer slept at home and had to exercise great circumspection to avoid arrest.

Towards the end of April 1960, a British lawyer arrived unannounced at my university office and told me that someone I knew, Vella Pillay of the London bureau of the Party, had sent him to make contact with the Central Committee, to offer assistance. Pillay assumed I could put them in touch. In fact I had dropped out of the Party some years earlier and did not know the whereabouts of the leadership. I told the visitor to hang around while I made enquiries. By chance, Wolfie Kodesh, whom I knew as a Party member, called on me the next day, saying that Harmel wanted to see me. I informed him of the arrival of the British visitor. Kodesh arranged a meeting with Harmel. Following this, I had a series of discussions with Harmel and Fischer, at their request. They told me that the emergency had found the Party totally unprepared. They asked me to become a lifeline between those in hiding and the outside world. I could not stand idly by at a time when the crisis engendered by Sharpeville seemed to present a real opportunity to challenge the regime. My ideological objections to the leadership's pro-Moscow line, and my dissatisfaction with their apparent isolation from the mass movement, which had led me to drop out of the Party a few years earlier, seemed irrelevant in circumstances where the whole movement was struggling to survive. With the benefit of hindsight this crossing of the Rubicon between my above-ground work in SACTU and as a lawyer and my active participation in illegal activities turned out to be a fundamental mistake.

I joined the third-tier Johannesburg district committee, helping to re-establish contacts with surviving groups and recruiting several new members who had shown their merit during the emergency. I was the contact for two trade union Party units and was elected chair of the district committee, a position to which I was twice re-elected until my arrest in July 1963. As chair, I was a member from May 1960 to July 1963 of the district secretariat, with Bartholomew Hlapane and Ben Turok, which carried out day-to-day work. In his memoir Turok recalls that '[Bob Hepple] was a highly intelligent and capable man whose involvement in the movement was not known and so he was able to join us in various meetings and discussions. He proved to be extremely reliable and his youthful fresh face was always welcome when he visited our little group.' Turok was imprisoned in 1962 for sabotage. Hlapane had become a full-time Party organiser in 1961. He was arrested shortly before the Rivonia raid in June 1963 and detained for 172 days. He was detained again in September 1964 and then 'cracked' and gave evidence in the Fischer trial and in a number of other trials, incidentally revealing for the first time my role as chair of the district committee. By this time I was out of the country. In 1981 he testified before a US Senate committee on 'communist subversion'. An MK unit executed him in 1983.

SACP emerges

In May 1960 an enlarged Central Committee meeting of those not in detention or exile was summoned to discuss the question of emergence. I was invited to attend the meeting held over two days, first in an artist's studio and then in open brickfields. About 12 to 15 people from Johannesburg, Durban, Port Elizabeth and Cape Town were present. There were different views about what was meant by 'emergence', and these rested on different understandings of the transition from capitalism to socialism. The dominant group within the Party asserted that the primary aim was 'national liberation' – it was necessary first to defeat the 'colonialism of a special type' represented by apartheid. This would be a democratic revolution including black capitalists, peasants and other groups, so as to create the conditions in which the Party could later agitate for socialism. This envisaged a fairly lengthy period before the communists won an electoral majority and introduced socialist measures. There were others in the Party (I believed a minority) who argued that it was possible to create the conditions for an immediate transition to socialism after overthrowing white domination. This required the dominance within the Congress alliance of the SACP as the 'vanguard' of the working class, openly advocating socialism. This was a Bolshevik model of revolution influenced by Leninist ideas.

After discussion it was unanimously agreed that the Party should emerge in its own name, embark on a recruiting campaign and bring out a regular newspaper. A number of organisational matters were discussed, including work in the now banned ANC and the other congresses. There were differences of opinion as to whether the emerged Party should aim to become a mass workers' and peasants' party or should remain a small body of 'professional revolutionaries' working mainly through the congresses. Moses Kotane was strongly in favour of the latter approach, and this won the day, largely on the practical ground that security considerations made a mass illegal organisation impossible.

Shortly after this meeting, I was co-opted onto the Central

Committee. The other members at the time were Kotane, Harmel, Turok, Fischer and Hlapane. The first task of the committee was to put into effect the resolution on emergence. After a few weeks a pamphlet was produced. Fischer and Kotane argued for a postponement. Fischer's objection was that the Treason Trial was still in progress and he feared that the pamphlet would damage the prospects for acquittal of those on trial. Kotane said it was necessary to prepare our allies. After prolonged discussion – lasting all night until 3 am – the decision was taken to bring out the leaflet. The majority consisted of Harmel, Turok, Hlapane and myself.

Units were prepared and eventually in June or July 1960 the leaflet announcing the Party was distributed in townships and factories. The event passed relatively unnoticed. The Party from time to time distributed an isiZulu-language pamphlet *Inkululeko* (Freedom) in its own name. A member, Aaron Molete, was arrested and charged under the Suppression of Communism Act for distributing this. I found myself briefed by Wolpe to appear for him. The only defence I could offer was the legalistic ground that the Communist Party of South Africa (CPSA), which was banned under the Act, was not the same as the SACP and so the charge was misconceived. Not surprisingly, this failed to convince the magistrate, who sentenced him to the maximum three years' imprisonment, saying that the offence was 'almost tantamount to high treason' and was more serious than any offence involving the ANC or PAC because 'the Communist Party has international ramifications'. When dismissing an appeal, the pro-regime sympathies of the presiding judge, Piet Cillie, a political appointment to the Bench, were shown. He mockingly asked me during legal argument whether I would be appointed minister of justice when the communists took over, because of my ingenuity! Molete's imprisonment on Robben

Island was the human price of emergence. It made the Party cautious about further public activities in its own name.

SACP's 'secret' resolution

There was little organised discussion of the options among members of the SACP and ANC regarding armed struggle before the end of 1960. The decision to embark on armed struggle was taken by a small leadership elite. An internal 'study document' written by Michael Harmel, with a title reminiscent of Lenin's famous pamphlet *What Is to Be Done?*, was circulated among SACP units. This claimed that the new 'total onslaught' by the government had set the movement on an inexorable path to violence, with little space for peaceful methods. Yet there were those, including Moses Kotane, general secretary of the SACP, who disagreed. When Mandela presented the case for armed struggle within the ANC working committee in June 1961, Kotane accused him of having not thought out the proposal carefully enough. Mandela recalls that Kotane said that 'I [Mandela] had been outmanoeuvred and paralysed by the government's actions and now in desperation was resorting to revolutionary language. "There is still room" [Kotane] stressed "for the old methods if we are imaginative and determined enough. If we embark on the course Mandela is suggesting, we will be exposing innocent people to massacres by the enemy."' In a private discussion with Kotane, Mandela told him that he was making the same mistake as the Communist Party of Cuba – 'they said the conditions for a revolution had not yet arrived', in line with the 'old methods' advocated by Lenin and Stalin as to how a revolutionary situation could be identified. Castro had proved them wrong, said Mandela, and had triumphed.

Kotane's fear that the time was not yet ripe for armed struggle sadly proved to be correct. What is significant about his stand in the ANC working committee is that six months earlier, in December 1960, a conference of the SACP attended by Kotane had resolved to establish military units and had instructed the Central Committee to take all necessary steps to that end. About 25 people attended the conference, including Mandela and Sisulu, Govan Mbeki, Ray Mhlaba, Dan Tloome, Ben Turok, John Nkadimeng, MP Naicker, Fred Carneson, Bram Fischer, Joe Slovo and Michael Harmel. Also present was Piet Beyleveld, who later turned to become a state witness against Fischer and other members of the Party. In all, there were eight delegates from the Johannesburg district committee and three each from Durban, Port Elizabeth and Cape Town. The remaining delegates were members of the Central Committee or chosen by that body. As described in chapter two, I had made all the technical and security arrangements for the conference and had been present for most of the sessions.

The conference had to sum up the lessons from the emergency period and, in the light of this, reassess the strategy and tactics of the Party. The business of the conference, over two days, was in three main parts: first, a report on the political situation by Bernstein; second, a report on Party organisation by Slovo; third, a report on the national liberation and trade union movements by Sisulu. There was also a report from Harmel, who had recently returned from a conference of communist parties in the Soviet Union, on the Sino-Soviet split. The first two reports were in the most general terms and the discussion on them was vague. The only really significant decision taken under the first item was the 'secret' resolution that was the real starting point of the armed struggle. It was agreed, without opposition, that the result of the emergency and the banning of the ANC was that a new phase had arrived, one in which a shift had to be made from legality to illegality as the main context of activity, and from non-violence to armed resistance as part of the struggle to overthrow the regime. The secret resolution was not recorded and not reported to members of the Party. Ben Turok recalls that the piece of paper on which the resolution was written was burned in front of the meeting and the ashes thrown through a trap door in the floor of the room, to highlight the seriousness of the decision, and we were all sworn to secrecy. I cannot recollect this and there is no mention of it in my notes made three years later, but Turok's account is entirely consistent with the atmosphere in which the issue was discussed. I do not remember any specific discussion about who would control the military units. In fact, such a discussion seemed unnecessary because it was taken for granted that the Party would directly control these units. My understanding was that the purpose of the units was to enable cadres to learn methods of armed resistance or, as some called it, 'armed propaganda'. The discussion was short and there was no suggestion at this time of full-scale guerrilla war. Bernstein claims that the decision was an interim one. There is no mention of this in my notes, but he and I are agreed that the discussion was short and the matter was referred to the Central Committee for further action.

While Kotane was willing to embrace some preparations for armed resistance, he was not in support of Mandela's far more ambitious yet vague plans. My recollection is that Mandela sat alongside Sisulu in the back row of seats in the room where the meeting was held but said little during the conference. I was told (I believe by Slovo) that Mandela had been invited as an observer. He was not one of the district committee delegates, nor had he been a member of the Central Committee during the time (up to December 1960) when I was co-opted to it. I do not know if he was co-opted to the Central Committee after the December 1960 conference. Several other members of the

Bob Hepple, c. 1963

Alex Hepple

Aunt Dolly (Dorothy Zwarenstein)

Girlie Hepple caring for Brenda and Paul after Bob and Shirley's escape, 1963

Hiking in Lesotho, 1953. (l to r) Beate Lipman, Charles Feinstein, our leader Eli Weinberg, Bob Hepple and Leon Levy

The last non-statutory Wits SRC, 1954-55. Those on the Student Liberal Association ticket included Ismail Mahomed, later Chief Justice (second row, second on right), Dan Goldstein (front row, second from left), Ruth Kaplan (née Baranov) who later worked with the human rights attorney Shulamith Muller (fourth from left), next to her Bob Hepple (President), and Sydney Shall, a Treason trialist (last on right)

Nelson Mandela, as I remember him on the first occasion we met in 1953

Mandela in traditional dress before his trial in 1962

Mandela being led to prison after his trial, 1962

Lilliesleaf farm in July 1963. The thatched cottage in which the main arrests took place on 11 July 1963 is at the top of the picture, the storerooms are next to this, and on the right is the room in which Mandela lived in 1961–2.

Top: Police photos of Walter Sisulu, Ahmed Kathrada, Govan Mbeki in their disguises.
Bottom: Rusty Bernstein, Denis Goldberg, Raymond Mhlaba.
(Historical Papers, Wits)

An unknown demonstrator
outside the South African
consulate in New York,
October 1963

'Rooi Rus' Swanepoel (extreme right)
looks on as the body of Babla Saloojee
is recovered, after he 'fell' from the 7th
floor of Security Police headquarters,
Johannesburg, September 1964

An unshaven Bob Hepple while
detained in solitary confinement.
Note the heavy eyelids and stare due
to sleep deprivation.

Bob and Shirley after arrival in Dar es Salaam, November 1963

Presentation of Labour Code, drafted by Bob Hepple, to (l to r) Minister of Labour Witbooi, President Nujoma, and Prime Minister Geingob of independent Namibia, April 1991

Old man with a red tie. Portrait of the Master of Clare College by Tomas Watson, 2001. The artist explains that the African fertility symbol in the background, brought from Ghana by Bob's wife, Mary Coussey, represents Bob's African past as well as the admission of women to Clare College which had been all-male for 650 years.

Party have claimed that he did become a member in 1960, and I recall one occasion in 1961 while he was in hiding when I took him with me as an observer to a meeting of the Johannesburg district committee held in a suburban house. He always publicly denied being a communist but acknowledged that he respected and worked closely with communist members of the ANC.

It was after the SACP's secret resolution that Mandela persuaded a tumultuous meeting of the National Executive Committee of the ANC, in June 1961, to establish a military organisation. It was agreed that this should be an independent body linked to but separate from the ANC, so as to protect the still-legal partners in the Congress alliance. Moreover, as Mandela recalls, 'armed struggle, at least in the beginning, would not be the centrepiece of the movement'. There was some opposition, notably from members of the Indian Congress. Mandela was authorised to go ahead and form Umkhonto weSizwe. The military units that the SACP had begun to set up under Slovo's leadership were merged into MK. The first sabotage attacks took place on 16 December 1961. Mandela acknowledges that 'we were embarking on a new and more dangerous path, a path of organised violence, the results of which we did not and could not know'.

At the Party conference in December 1960 there was a discussion about whether a new legal body should be created to replace the ANC or whether the ANC should instead continue underground. Sisulu and Mandela were firmly wedded to maintaining the ANC, which they believed had high prestige and authority among the people. They also regarded as illusory the hope that another legal front organisation could survive. The suggestion that the underground SACP should be built up into a mass organisation was instantly rejected as 'dangerously sectarian'. My own view, shared with some delegates and based on my experience in SACTU, was that there was still a huge potential for recruitment and activity by the trade unions, despite the severe restrictions under which they operated. Organised workers could exert huge economic pressure. Some of us thought that this task of organising the urban working class should take priority. The setting up of armed units in the townships and rural areas to protect people from police attacks and to harass the authorities was necessary, but should be regarded as a secondary activity. However, over the next two years the preparation by an elite for armed struggle became the dominant activity.

At the December 1960 conference I was not elected or co-opted onto the new Central Committee. I was retained as a member of the Johannesburg district committee and was re-elected as its chair. We set ourselves the task of recruiting more factory workers, mainly in the trade unions, who were expected to be cadres leading mass working-class activity. By July 1963, Party membership in Johannesburg was about 225, double the number in 1960. The activities of these members remained much the same as before the emergence of the Party in 1960, the Party line being that members must dedicate themselves to day-to-day work in the Congress organisations.

'The Road to South African Freedom'

The emergence of the Party made it necessary to have a programme. At the beginning of 1962 a draft programme was circulated among units. There had been a short statement of aims when the SACP was formed in 1953. Most members had never seen that statement or, if they had, had forgotten the contents. I was told that Harold Wolpe had a strong role in developing the idea that white domination was a form of 'internal colonialism' in the draft programme called 'The Road to South African Freedom'. Units were asked to study the draft, which was accompanied by study guides and a reading list, and to submit comments and suggested amendments. Police raids caused many units to destroy their copy of the draft before they had discussed it, and one or two copies actually fell into police hands. I had the opportunity to discuss the draft with two units consisting entirely of manual workers. They found the draft incomprehensible because of the use of academic concepts, which I tried to explain to them in simpler language.

I had the task of reading and summarising all the comments made by units in Johannesburg. I was appointed a member of the committee to revise the draft and present a report to a conference at which the programme was to be adopted. I played a minor role on the committee, which was dominated by the Party heavyweights, Michael Harmel and Moses Kotane. We met, usually at my home, over a period of three weeks in August and September 1962. The document produced by the committee was full of communist rhetoric, some borrowed from Marx and Engels's *Communist Manifesto of 1848,* and some from documents of the international conference of communist parties that Harmel had attended in 1960. The programme stated that the 'immediate and foremost task' was to work for 'a united front of national liberation ... for a national democratic revolution to destroy white domination ... [T]his revolution will at the same time put an end to every sort of racial discrimination and privilege. The revolution will restore the land and the wealth of the country to the people, and guarantee democracy, freedom and equality of rights and opportunities for all.' It said that 'the destruction of colonialism and the winning of national freedom is the essential condition and the key for future advance to the supreme aim of the Communist Party: the establishment of a socialist South Africa, laying the foundation of a classless, communist society'. The wording was ambiguous – some would say superficial enough – to bridge the gap between those who envisaged a rapid transition to socialism and those who did not.

In October 1962, the Central Committee convened a national conference, at a safe house in Johannesburg, primarily to adopt the new programme, and to elect a new Central Committee. The conference was called at very short notice because of the threats of imminent house arrest of a number of leaders. This resulted in units not having the opportunity to submit resolutions on topical issues. I attended as a representative of the Johannesburg district committee. The first morning was devoted to reading the new draft (for security reasons it had not been circulated in advance) and to a preliminary discussion. The second and third sessions on the same day heard a political report. A number of delegates were compelled to leave at the end of the first day – the first house arrests had been imposed and a report was received that the police were looking for Sisulu and some others who were not at home because of the conference. It was resolved to send them home so as to reduce the intense police activity. Unfortunately this meant that the conference was deprived of delegates who could have made a significant contribution.

On one topic there was a heated debate. This was Transkeian 'independence'. The majority view was that the fraud of self-governance must be exposed by boycotting the dummy Legislative Council elections, while a vocal minority thought that the correct strategy was to form an alliance with the government's opponents on the Legislative Council. There was also a third standpoint, that the basic question was how to prepare the people in the rural areas for guerrilla warfare and to turn these areas into guerrilla bases. For this purpose, it was said, the people should be politicised before, during and after an election campaign, but that little emphasis should be placed on securing representation on the Council. Eventually a resolution was adopted reflecting the majority view. The Legislative Council elections later took place without Party or Congress participation.

The second day was spent discussing the programme, which was unanimously adopted by the 25 to 30 persons present. One of the striking features of the conference was the number of young and enthusiastic African delegates from the Western and Eastern Cape. They were articulate and brought a hopeful, militant and determined approach to the conference. I was appointed a scrutineer for the Central Committee elections, which were held under new rules that allowed for seven out of the 13 seats to be elected by secret ballot at the conference. The names of those elected were not announced. They were Moses Kotane, Walter Sisulu, JB Marks, MP Naicker, Govan Mbeki, Joe Slovo and Rusty Bernstein. I learned later that they immediately co-opted Duma Nokwe, Mark Shope, Michael Harmel, Bram Fischer, Ruth First, Fred Carneson and Bartholomew Hlapane. I was not elected to the Central Committee but was co-opted in April 1963 after the house arrests multiplied and several members of the committee were sent abroad.

The SACP and MK
I was never recruited into the Party's military units, which merged with those of the ANC to form MK some time in 1961. I was, however, aware that trade union and Party cadres were disappearing, apparently for military training. The Johannesburg district committee was out of the loop, remaining ignorant of the structure of the new military organisation and who controlled it, and the preparations for sabotage. We were informed that the SACP and ANC each had four representatives on the High Command but their identities were secret. On 16 December 1961 a few small acts of sabotage were committed and

some units of the Party were used to distribute a 'proclamation' announcing the existence of MK, described as a military sabotage organisation that accepted the guidance of the national liberation organisations. The 'proclamation' – as the police later proved – turned out to have been typed on an SACP typewriter, so that all the attempts made to distance the Party from MK appeared to be mildly ridiculous. The period from June 1961 to July 1963 saw the Party 'submerge' as MK grew.

As a result of protests by the district committee about the sudden disappearance of members, a plan was agreed whereby MK would inform the district secretariat of the name of any person who had been recruited and sent abroad for military training. Members of the Party were told that if they were approached to join MK, for security reasons they should not discuss this with their unit or other Party members. The effect was that the Party became subordinate to the new military organisation at a time when armed resistance was still regarded by many of us as secondary to more traditional forms of struggle, including trade union activity. I remember my shock and disappointment when I was informed that two leading trade unionists and Party members, who had been doing indispensable trade union work, had been 'pulled out' for MK activities. This information came not from the Central Committee to me as a member of the district secretariat but directly from the High Command of MK. When I spoke to the individuals concerned they explained that they had been reluctant to give up their union activities but, unable to consult the Party, they feared that if they declined the invitation to join MK they would be considered 'disloyal'. After hearing from them, I exerted heavy pressure on the High Command, which then released them from MK to return to trade union work.

In the period before April 1963, I did not know what control, if any, the Central Committee exercised over MK. After the sabotage campaign started, some Party members, who were not also in MK, began to complain about the 'amateurism' of sabotage attacks, which had resulted in the accidental death of Petrus Molefe, an MK volunteer, and the arrest of others, including Turok. Mandela says that 'Molefe's death indicated … that we had not sufficiently trained people, and it was something very disturbing. But … you can't avoid casualties when you are starting a new method of political activity.' Turok describes the 'amateurishness and bungling' of the operation to plant a bomb in the Rissik Street Post Office, which led to his arrest and imprisonment for three years. More significantly, it seemed that individual acts of sabotage were being substituted for organised political activity. The district committee had a stream of reports that the ANC as an organisation was all but dead. The 'seven-person' structure of basic ANC units underground had failed to work; members of these groups kept away from meetings, and leaflets produced at great risk lay undistributed. The residents' associations formed as legal fronts for the ANC and SACP disintegrated because of rivalries and factions. However, there was some increase in trade union membership, showing the importance and potential of this aspect of the struggle, but SACTU as a coordinating body was badly hit by bannings and arrests. The sabotage attacks gave the government the excuse to mount its 'total onslaught', including vicious new counter-sabotage laws and detention without trial. Torture and other forms of state terrorism became routine. The movement was caught unprepared.

Operation Mayibuye

When I joined the secretariat of the Central Committee in April 1963, I did not know who were members of the High Command of MK, who were on the ANC National Executive Committee and who, like me, were operating only within the structures of the Party. We functioned on a 'need to know' basis, so I did not ask. Fischer told me that the High Command of MK had decided to send Slovo and JB Marks to Dar es Salaam to present a plan for guerrilla warfare – called Operation Mayibuye – to the external leadership. He stressed that the internal ANC and SACP bodies had neither seen nor adopted the plan. He was very unhappy about this. The High Command of MK had jumped the gun – it had been agreed when MK was set up that a shift from acts of sabotage to guerrilla war would take place only after full consultation with the leadership of the ANC and SACP, and that had not happened.

A meeting was called for the morning of Saturday 6 July in the main farmhouse at Lilliesleaf. There were about a dozen people present. In addition to the secretariat, these included Fischer, Ruth First and Hlapane. They were all Party members but I did not know what positions, if any, they also held in MK or the ANC. The 'Operation Mayibuye' document was not circulated but its main contents were briefly explained. These were already familiar to most of those present but were new to me. It was a plan for full-scale guerrilla war. Hundreds of activists would leave the country to be trained in organising and leading a guerrilla struggle. They would, with the help of friendly African states, return with arms and explosives to a number of pre-selected areas. In the meantime a network of at least 7000 full-time organisers would prepare these areas politically and organisationally, and be ready to join the guerrilla army in its initial onslaught. This would be accompanied by campaigns of mass mobilisation, including a national anti-pass campaign, to cause an upheaval throughout the country. There were detailed organisational plans for the implementation of this strategy.

The meeting was deeply divided. Mbeki and Mhlaba were

FROM 'OPERATION MAYIBUYE'

The white state has thrown overboard every pretence of rule by democratic process. Armed to the teeth it has presented the people with only one choice and that is to its overthrow by force and violence. It can now truly be said that very little, if any, scope exists for the smashing of white supremacy other than by means of mass revolutionary action, the main content of which is armed resistance leading to victory by military means ... We are confident that the masses will respond in overwhelming numbers to a lead which holds out a real possibility of successful armed struggle.

... [T]wo important ingredients of a revolutionary situation are present:-
(a) A disillusionment with constitutional or semi-constitutional forms of struggle and a conviction that the road to victory is through force; (b) A militancy and readiness to respond to a lead which holds out a real possibility of successful struggle.

In the light of the existence of these ingredients the prosecution of military struggle depends for it success on two further factors:-
(a) The strength of the enemy. This must not be looked at statically but in the light of objective factors, which in a period of military struggle may well expose its brittleness and
(b) The existence of a clear leadership with material resources at its disposal to spark off and sustain military operations. The objective military conditions in which the movements

115

[sic] finds itself makes the possibility of a general uprising leading to direct military struggle an unlikely one. Rather, as in Cuba, the general uprising must be sparked off by organised and well-prepared guerrilla operations during the course of which the masses of the people will be drawn in and armed …

Although we must prepare for a protracted war we must not lose sight of the fact that the political isolation of South Africa from the world community of nations and particularly the active hostility towards it from almost the whole of the African Continent and the socialist world may result in such massive resistance in various forms, that the state structure will collapse far sooner than we can at this moment envisage …

The following plan envisages a process which will place in the field, at a date fixed now, simultaneously in pre-selected areas armed and trained guerella [sic] bands who will find ready to join them local guerella bands with arms and equipment at their disposal. It will further coincide with a massive propaganda campaign both inside and outside South Africa and a general call for unprecedented mass struggle throughout the land, both violent and non-violent …

We are convinced that this plan is capable of fulfilment … The time for small thinking is over because history leaves us no choice …

enthusiastic supporters of the plan, as (we were told) was Slovo. In his posthumously published memoir, Slovo acknowledges that 'hindsight, that most infallible (and sometimes irritating) critic, will surely demonstrate how utterly unreal our expectations were … Not for the first time in the history of radical struggle did the optimism of will displace the pessimism of intelligence leading, at best, to an heroic failure.' They believed that armed invasion and guerrilla warfare were the only way to defeat the regime. They were inspired by Castro's success in Cuba. One hundred and twelve men had left Mexico in an unseaworthy boat, *Granma*, and landed in Cuba. All except 12 (including Castro and Guevara) were either killed or captured. But within 18 months these 12 marched into Havana at the head of a 10,000-strong guerrilla army and overthrew Batista.

Sisulu, however, was equivocal. He felt that guerrilla warfare was probably not a feasible option at this stage. Ruth First was also ambivalent. Fischer, on the other hand, described the plan as utterly unrealistic and gave a number of practical reasons why it could not succeed. He said that it could lead only to disaster. At his subsequent trial Fischer described Operation Mayibuye as 'the most impractical and ridiculous plan'. Bernstein made the most detailed political critique, saying that the plan proceeded from a wholly mistaken analysis of the balance of power in the country and of the strengths and weaknesses of the government and the movement. He put forward a possible alternative plan for limited guerrilla activities, in the form of quick attacks on border outposts and retreat into bases in the British Protectorates, leading to an international incident, which could precipitate national strikes and a serious political crisis. The only alternative to this, he said, was a protracted guerrilla war, which was unlikely to succeed because of the might of the South African state and its backers.

Kathrada was also opposed to the plan. He commented many years later that his comrades in hiding at Lilliesleaf 'were living in a world of their own, completely divorced from reality. Theirs was a world of fantasy, romanticism, impatience and intolerance, but the problem was, they sincerely believed in what they were writing and planning. They were in a hurry to implement it, and did not take kindly to any criticism.' I said little during the meeting, being the youngest and greenest member, but I agreed with the political objections raised by Bernstein and the practical ones raised by Fischer. I thought it was a crazy plan which would provoke brutal repression and set back by years what I regarded as the main task, that of building up effective political and trade union organisation among the people. This was not Batista's fragile and corrupt Cuba but a highly armed state, supported by the white population and backed by the USA as part of its global strategy against the Soviet Union, which was supporting the liberation movement. A military operation of the kind envisaged had no hope of success and would result in untold suffering.

The debate could not be concluded on that Saturday morning because Bernstein had to get home by 2 pm in order to comply with his house arrest order. We then arranged the fatal meeting of the secretariat for the following Thursday 11 July. That morning First came to my house and asked me to give some messages to Sisulu and Mbeki. We had become close personal and political confidants, especially since the departure of her husband, Slovo, for Dar es Salaam at the end of May. So we soon fell into conversation about Operation Mayibuye. She saw the dangers but brushed them aside on the grounds that 'for the first time in years we are getting things done'. She was highly impressed by the efficiency and resolve of the MK men, compared with the endless, tiresome committee meetings of the political organisations. I voiced my concerns that decisions being taken by the MK High Command were bleeding the unions and other organisations of some of their most important activists. By recruiting those engaged in the 'legal' struggle, MK's High Command was violating the basic rule, which had been adopted at an early stage, that there should be a strict separation between those doing legal work – such as in trade unions – and those directly engaged in illegal military activities. It was a joke, which she and I shared, that we were now under 'military dictatorship'. The bitter fruits were to be reaped in the following months and years.

Personal doubts

My conversation with Ruth had renewed my long-standing doubts about what I was doing. Could I continue to expose myself to grave dangers if Operation Mayibuye, with which I profoundly disagreed, was adopted? While I wanted to help the political leaders of the African people, and understood the reasons why they had turned to armed resistance, I had never seen myself as cut out for this kind of activity. What strengths I had to contribute were as a lawyer, writer, speaker and lecturer, and union activist, but certainly not a revolutionary soldier. I felt torn between Ruth's infectious sense of urgency and my enormous respect for the political sagacity of the collective leadership, on the one hand, and my deep personal unease with the direction they were taking, on the other. Now I was in detention and the police had all the evidence they needed to convict and sentence me for a plan to which I had never subscribed.

How long, I thought, as I tossed and turned through the next few nights in the isolation of my cell, will all these secrets be safe with me? How long can I withstand interrogation? I need to ensure that Fischer and others still outside the police net remain safe and that the police do not discover our remaining safe houses. If I can secure my release quickly, by making a statement that the police find credible, I think, I can grab the opportunity to ensure that other hiding places are cleared out and pass on messages to Fischer and others. Even if I am not immediately released, an innocent explanation now might be used in evidence at any trial and so help my defence. This would be a gamble because I did not know how much evidence about me the police had gathered, who was talking and what they were saying. To make a statement would be to break a basic rule that one should not cooperate with the police, but were these not extraordinary circumstances, when any chance of freedom should be taken?

Chapter Six

INTERROGATION
August–September 1963

The first statement

On the weekend of 3 and 4 August a miracle occurs. The usual warders are away. The relief warders – apparently unaware of the restrictions on communication between the political detainees – turn their backs on us. At first we cannot believe it, then we start excited whispers, which become a full conversation for nearly half an hour. I am able to talk to Bernstein during the exercise period. We are also able to pass notes to each other. The consensus that emerges is that if I can get out quickly by making a statement giving an innocuous reason for my presence at Lilliesleaf, I should grab the opportunity. We are not able to discuss the contents of the proposed statement in detail. But we agree that I should say that we had come to consider the position of 90-day detainees, and were not discussing anything else when the police arrived.

I will not make a statement at that stage without Bernstein's agreement. He has known me since I was a boy and I trust him as a friend and senior comrade. He has many years of underground experience, and so can judge what might work. I manage to talk briefly to Goldberg as well. Unlike Bernstein, he does not know the degree of my involvement – 11 July was the first time our paths had crossed – nor do I know his. He says he does not object to the course I am taking, but warns me that it could be dangerous. Bernstein says the risk is worth taking. At that stage we have no contact with the outside world. We do not know who has been arrested and what finds have been made, apart from the discovery of Mandela's documents and other records at Lilliesleaf. I believe that I have the consent of all those whom it is possible for me to consult to make a statement to the police.

On Monday 5 August, Swanepoel and D/Sgt. Van Zyl call on me. I make a statement, typed out by Swanepoel in response to leading questions by Van Zyl. The gist of this statement is that I have been a member of the Congress of Democrats, that I got to know Sisulu in this period, and that I had acted as his lawyer on a few occasions. On the morning of 11 July I had received a message from Sisulu asking to come and see him in hiding at Lilliesleaf to discuss 90-day detention and to advise him about his appeal against his conviction in the regional court. I had agreed to go, and had received instructions from an Indian man (whose name I did not know) that morning as to how to find Lilliesleaf. I had arrived at Rivonia at 3 pm and seen a car leaving. The mention of my visitor and the car leaving is intended to test my suspicions as to the informant. I state that I was surprised to find others there in addition to Sisulu, and had been there for only a short time before the police raided.

The second statement

After I make this statement, Van Zyl brushes it aside, and he and Swanepoel proceed for many hours to subject me to an incredible barrage of intimidation, threats and promises. They say they have inside informants – they know I have been to Lilliesleaf many times. They say they have statements from witnesses that I have been a member of a communist cell. Shirley will be detained until I tell the truth. I was using a car registered in my father's name when I came to Lilliesleaf, so he must be implicated and he and my mother will be detained. My parents-in-law are communist sympathisers and they will be detained. My children will go to an orphanage. I will never be released. I will be hanged with all the others …

During all of this I am kept standing in front of the desk where Swanepoel and Van Zyl are sitting, not allowed to sit down or go to the toilet. My mind and body are exhausted, but I simply maintain that my statement is true. Eventually, I am taken back to my cell. That night warders or police (I am not sure which) keep coming into my cell, unlocking and locking the door, shouting and depriving me of sleep.

For the next three days interrogation by various policemen continues in the same way for hours on end. There are only short breaks. I lose all track of time. One of Swanepoel's ploys is to leave a revolver on the desk, then pick it up and play Russian roulette after showing me the one bullet: 'Would you like this or the rope?' he says. The threats and promises are distorted out of all proportion in my mind, and my capacity to reason is seriously impaired. I say this with the wisdom of hindsight, because one of the consequences of sensory deprivation and exhaustion is that one is unable to realise the extent of the changes taking place in normal behaviour. I am not taken out during exercise periods and have no opportunity to communicate with either Bernstein or Goldberg.

During another sleepless night on 8 August, I decide that I will have to make a more incriminating statement if I am to have any hope of release. Swanepoel has made a promise that if I give a satisfactory statement, he will take me to Langlaagte police station in Johannesburg, where conditions will be easier. I know the station. It is near the main road, and security might be lax enough for me to escape. By now I have convinced myself that if I make a credible statement I will either be released – as Swanepoel and Van Zyl repeatedly promise – or at least will be moved to Langlaagte and have a chance to escape.

The following day, when questioning resumes at the prison, I say I will make a statement. I am taken to The Grays. I make a statement in response to questions by Swanepoel and a number of police officers. I have to tread the fine line of making a statement that is credible but does not incriminate any of my comrades who have been arrested or may still be in the country. I admit that I was recruited into the Communist Party in 1954. I say that this was by Advocate Joe Slovo. He is out of the country. I am protecting Harold Wolpe, who in fact recruited me, because I do not know whether or not he is still at large. I say (truthfully) that I allowed my membership to lapse, but on 11 July 1963 I was again a member. I make this admission not only because they claim to have statements of informers to this effect, but also because their interrogation has made it obvious that they know that I would not have been invited to the secret hiding place if I were not a member of the Party.

I say (truthfully) that in about October 1962 Slovo had asked me to receive correspondence at my office address for the 'movement'. I know from the interrogation that the police have found at Lilliesleaf some envelopes addressed to 'Cedric' from 'Natalie', so there is no use denying this. I also suspect that the Indian man who had used these code names when he visited me on the morning of 11 July was a police spy.

I say (truthfully) that at first I had given the letters I received to Slovo, but that later I had taken them there on my own. This is intended to tie in with the witness statements they undoubtedly have from farm workers that I have been seen at Lilliesleaf on several occasions. I say that Slovo took me out to the farm for the first time in about April 1963. I am concealing my knowledge of Mandela's stay there and any information about my visits to Lilliesleaf before April 1963. I say that I have seen Slovo, Mbeki, Sisulu, Kathrada and Bernstein at the farm when delivering messages. I am concealing all my knowledge of their functioning as the secretariat, of its meetings, and of the meeting on 6 July – none of these is mentioned. I say that on one or two occasions I drove to the farm with Kathrada and took him back to the city (this was because they say I have been seen coming in and out with him). I say I do not know Goldberg (who was introduced to me as 'Williams'). I say I have met Goldreich there once or twice. Other names are put to me, such as First, Mandela, Festenstein, Kantor and Wolpe, but I say that I have never seen any of them at Lilliesleaf, nor do I know anything about their activities. At one point, the police say that they have reliable information that Fischer is the 'head' of the Communist Party. I deny all knowledge of this.

I am subjected to intensive questioning about what was discussed, and say that in my presence it was only the 90-day detentions, the provisions of the Sabotage Act, Sisulu's appeal, the defence of persons charged with political offences, and related matters that were discussed. I deny all knowledge of Operation Mayibuye. I say that there were various documents lying about in the room, but I do not know their contents. I say that I was never told what activities were being conducted from Lilliesleaf, and was actively discouraged from knowing what they were doing. I believe that nothing in that statement gave the police more information than they already had, or incriminated anyone else inside the country.

Escape thwarted
After the questioning on 9 August I am taken to Langlaagte

police station. I have a large but dark and cold cell near the main road. There is a high wall in my private exercise yard, and I start working on a plan to scale the wall (the cell door into the yard is left open at night). If I can get a message out to have a car waiting for me near the main road, I may be able to escape. I spend my 29th birthday on 11 August there. I am cheered by a brief visit by Shirley, who has been allowed to see me. She brings me fish and chips which she has cleverly wrapped in that morning's *Sunday Times.* The headlines say that Goldreich, Wolpe and two other men have escaped from Marshall Square police station. The door of the waiting room in which Shirley and I are meeting is open and I can see through to the reception desk and the main road. Could I just run out at that moment? That will get Shirley into trouble. We have not had time to make plans, so it would end in a fiasco. While I am thinking of this, the police constable announces that our time is up and I am escorted back to my cell. The door from my cell to the yard is securely locked behind me. I am taken back to Pretoria on 14 August. There has been a security crackdown as a result of Goldreich and Wolpe's escape. There is now no way that I can escape or expect release.

The impossibility of an escape is brought home by the experience of Goldberg in late August. I no longer see him in the exercise yard. He reappears later shackled in leg irons. I learn that he had been taken to Vereeniging Prison from which he tried to escape. He was quickly recaptured. When he was being transferred back to Pretoria, a warder had cut into his leg with a hacksaw while removing rivets from the leg irons, causing bleeding. The first inkling that those outside get of this escape is when Shirley collects his washing (as she does for all the detainees each week) and finds bloodstains. She raises the alarm. In fact, Goldberg is not seriously hurt, but his failed attempt shows me how hopeless it would be to plan an escape.

This simply adds to my deep depression after being returned to Pretoria. The endless, boring days in solitary confinement continue. My ploy in making a statement on 9 August has compromised me. I fear that my admissions are enough to link me to the common purpose of the MK High Command, and at the very least have made me liable for supporting the activities of unlawful organisations. I was not able to escape from Langlaagte police station, I cannot escape from Pretoria prison, and my belief that I will be released is a forlorn hope.

After about a fortnight back in Pretoria, Bernstein passes me a note he has received from outside. It says they are worried about me having made a statement. Did I realise it might later be used against me? Bernstein and I pass each other notes. He says that even if we had been wrong, which he does not think is the case, the results will not be disastrous. I am less optimistic and come to regret what I now believe was a serious error of judgement made while I was unable to think straight. I had put myself in a false position by volunteering the first statement, then had been psychologically and physically pressured into incriminating myself. The mere fact that I have made a statement will be used to demoralise others. I begin to feel ashamed.

Are you a Jewboy?

The first inkling of what is in store for me comes when Van Zyl and Swanepoel visit me. In a casual fashion Swanepoel says that '*daardie kwaai Jewboy*' (that angry Jewboy) Dr Percy Yutar, the deputy attorney-general who is to prosecute the Rivonia accused, has said that the only way out for me is to become a state witness. I will not be released unless I testify. 'You're a bloody Jewboy, too, aren't you?' Swanepoel asks aggressively.

The police are obsessed with showing that all the white men

caught at Rivonia – Bernstein, Goldberg, Goldreich, Wolpe, Festenstein and I – are Jewish communists. The warders follow suit. When Colonel Aucamp makes his rounds of the white detainees' cells, he says, 'Good morning Jew, good morning communist!', as if you cannot be a communist unless you are a Jew, and if you are a Jew you are a communist. The warder, whom I described as a 'fascist shit' in the note written on toilet paper found in my cell, stares at me as I take a cold shower. He exclaims incredulously, '*Nie besny!*' – Not circumcised! – and mockingly asks, '*Was jy nie by die kafferskool?*' – Weren't you at the 'kaffer' school? – the derogatory term used to denote tribal circumcision schools, which he likens to Jewish circumcision.

The fact is that I have a maternal Dutch Jewish heritage, but was not brought up as a Jew. My mother's family did not practise any religion, but were a family of 'Jews without Judaism' (the term applied to Baruch Spinoza, the Dutch philosopher, who denied that Jews were the 'chosen' people). Oupa Zwarenstein called himself a 'freethinker'. My father was a lapsed Catholic. I was brought up without synagogue or church and have no religious belief. But Swanepoel's question recalls for me the fate of my Dutch relatives in the Holocaust. I respond: 'Yes, if it matters, I am.'

What I found particularly puzzling as I grew up was the apparent ease with which most South African Jews, whose families had fled from pogroms in Russia, Lithuania, Latvia and Germany, fell in with the racial prejudices and loyalties of other white South Africans. Dan Jacobson wrote that 'as the result of their upbringing in a passionately colour-conscious society, South African Jews in general actually share all the colour prejudices of their fellow whites'. This was despite the discrimination against Jews. When I joined a horse-riding school at the age of 13, there was a notice, 'Gentiles only', which I ignored. Many golf and tennis clubs had similar rules. The Afrikaner press used the figure of 'Hoggenheimer' – a caricature of Sir Ernest Oppenheimer, the diamond and gold magnate – as symbol of a 'British-Jewish' capitalist conspiracy; there were moves to curb Jewish immigration in Acts of 1930 and 1936; and in 1933 a South African Gentile Nationalist movement was founded and assumed Nazi trappings. Dr Verwoerd (later prime minister) identified a 'Jewish problem' and his party for some years excluded Jews from membership. Jews made up about only four per cent of the white population in the 1950s and 1960s (166,000). The Nationalist attitude to this community changed after their election to power in 1948 and the foundation of the Jewish state of Israel. I heard Paul Sauer, a South African cabinet minister, say: 'I am a Zionist – I would like all the Jews to go to Israel!' The ban on membership of the National Party was lifted in 1951 and the Jewish vote for the Nationalists increased in the 1953 and 1958 elections. When Israel supported a strong resolution against apartheid at the United Nations in 1961, Verwoerd said, 'This is a tragedy for Jewry in South Africa', and the fact that so many Jews had favoured the anti-Nationalist Progressive Party 'did not pass unnoticed'. He lashed out at Israel, saying that the Jews had taken the land from the Arabs who had lived there for a thousand years: 'In that I agree with them. Israel, like South Africa, is an apartheid state.' In the 1970s and 1980s, Israel maintained strong ties with apartheid South Africa, supplying expertise and equipment and collaborating in the nuclear field. Most Jews knew of the anti-semitism in the National Party and that Verwoerd's motives were to maintain white unity, but the Jewish Board of Deputies waited on Verwoerd to congratulate him when he declared a white republic and heaped praise on him when he was murdered in 1966. They believed that by so doing they were protecting the Jewish community. There were, however, Jews who became activists against apartheid. Some fought within the system: parliamentarians like Leo Lovell and Hymie Davidoff of the Labour Party and Helen Suzman of the Progressive Party, trade unionists such as Solly Sachs and Ray Alexander, lawyers like Israel ('Isie') Maisels and Sydney Kentridge in the Treason Trial, and Arthur Chaskalson and Joel Joffe in the Rivonia Trial. There were others who exposed the system through the power of literature and theatre, like Nadine Gordimer, Dan Jacobson, Barney Simon, Janet Suzman and Anthony Sher. The most radical were communists who joined the armed struggle, such as Joe Slovo and Ronnie Kasrils, and others, such as Eli Weinberg, Norman Levy, and Esther and Hymie Barsel, who were imprisoned for Communist Party activities. The truth is that most white socialists and communists were, in Isaac Deutscher's phrase, 'non-Jewish Jews'; they 'had a universalism that left little space for ethnic particularism', in the words of the historians of South African Jewry. Some Russian and Lithuanian Jewish immigrants combined this with a passionate devotion to the Soviet Union, which they viewed as the liberator of Jews from centuries of oppression, and steadfastly refused to believe any of the stories circulating about anti-semitism in the communist countries. When six of the nine doctors accused of plotting against Stalin in 1953 turned out to be Jewish, I heard Jewish Soviet sympathisers claim that this was evidence of a 'Zionist conspiracy' rather than anti-semitism.

The fact is that South African Jews behaved in a variety of ways towards apartheid. I was now to meet a Jew who identified with and benefited from white supremacy. This was Dr Percy Yutar, the state prosecutor in the Rivonia Trial, who was determined to punish those Jews who had stepped out of line.

Dr Yutar

A few days after Swanepoel's visit I am taken to The Grays, the security police building where Dr Yutar has established his office. This is my first outing since being returned to Pretoria in August. After being kept waiting for a long time, I am called into Yutar's office. He is a short, balding, middle-aged man. I have seen him once or twice in action as a prosecutor. As a young and inexperienced advocate I hold him in awe. In court he is articulate, well prepared, rarely referring to his notes, and effectively uses irony and sarcasm to undermine the credibility of defence witnesses. He is always referred to as 'Dr' in recognition of his doctorate in law, a rather unusual distinction for an advocate. He adopts a somewhat obsequious manner towards judges, which endears him to them. My cousin Fred Zwarenstein has often crossed swords with him forensically and has told me about his ruthlessness and reluctance to make plea bargains. Yutar knows the Zwarenstein family because his father, was, like Oupa Zwarenstein, a butcher – indeed, his left hand was mangled in an electric mincing machine, leaving him with a permanent disability.

Without any introductions and keeping me standing, he immediately launches into a fierce attack on all the Jews who are 'communists' and proceeds to deliver a lecture, in an agitated falsetto voice, as to why, as a Jew, I should save myself, my family and the Jews in South Africa by agreeing to be a state witness. I reply that I had been promised release if I made a statement. He says there is no way I will get out without giving evidence. 'I'm going to prosecute you. All of you can expect to be sentenced to death.' With that threat he sends me out of the room.

The summary of evidence

The 'soft' Lt. Van Wyk takes me aside. 'I have pleaded with

Yutar to let you go, but he refuses to do so. The only way out now is for you to be a state witness.' I reply, 'I'll have to think about it, and consult others.' What is now going through my mind is the possibility of conditional release pending being called as a witness, which would enable me to escape. I know that I will never actually testify against the accused – that is unthinkable. I need more time to think about what is involved. Van Wyk pulls out a typewriter and I agree, with promptings and further questions from him, to type out a 'summary of evidence'. This more or less repeats in the form of a witness statement the information I gave during the interrogation on 9 August. It is eight pages long. I do not sign it. (The statement was recovered from Dr Yutar's files many years later and is now in the National Archives with other Rivonia Trial materials. The document has a number of underlinings, presumably made by Yutar, and at the end a handwritten note, 'summary of evidence 11.9.63'.)

Had I succeeded in being sufficiently economical with the truth so as not to harm my comrades? My statement says nothing about preparations for the armed struggle, or Operation Mayibuye, or the plans of the SACP and ANC. The Rivonia accused were subsequently convicted entirely on the basis of other overwhelming evidence, not my statement. In his memoir Bernstein says that 'any testimony [Hepple] can give can have little significance in the case against us'.

After this summary of evidence has been typed, I am taken back to Pretoria prison and remain there until the end of September.

Chapter Seven

OUTWITTING THE ENEMY
October 1963

The dilemma

I am kept in isolation from the other detainees in a cell on the first floor of Pretoria Local near to the cells of three convicted political prisoners, Ben Turok, Jack Tarshish and Harold Strachan, of whom I catch glimpses in their prison garb. I am taken out of my cell to the exercise yard on my own, and so have no opportunity to communicate clandestinely or otherwise with Bernstein, whose advice I badly need. Shall I take the gamble and agree to be a state witness on condition that I am released? This would give me an opportunity to escape. Or should I refuse point-blank, knowing that I will then face trial with the others or renewed detention without trial?

On 1 October I am taken back to The Grays. This time it is not the friendly Van Wyk but Swanepoel, red in the face in an aggressive mood, with Van Zyl and another security man. They tell me that they now have a statement from an informant that Fischer is the head of the underground and that Slovo, Wolpe and I are his 'chief lieutenants'. I dismiss this as complete nonsense. Yutar then calls me in to his office. He says five or six 'leading persons' are making statements and he wants to see what they have to say about me before he takes any further decision. I am kept at Langlaagte police station for the last week of my detention. It is an anxious time. If any 'leading person' is talking, there is a real danger I will be implicated and my statement will be dismissed as a cover-up.

On Monday 7 October, I am taken back to Yutar. He says he has decided to use me as a witness. I have still not been able to speak to anyone for advice. I say I want to consult the Johannesburg Bar Council and my family. Advocates Nicholas and Schwartz of the Bar Council come immediately to see me. They are sympathetic, but not unexpectedly they advise me that if I give evidence implicating myself, the Bar Council might feel obliged to move to disbar me so as to avoid having the minister accuse them of conniving in subversion. I am also allowed to meet Shirley and my mother, and manage to smuggle to them a copy of my typewritten statement. 'Get this to Bram [Fischer],' I say, which they do.

Later my father arrives accompanied by Israel Maisels QC, who successfully defended Mandela and others in the Treason Trial. As chair of the Treason Trial Defence Fund my father had come to know him well. Maisels had successfully advised my father when (the then Major) Van den Bergh had sued him for alleged defamation in an interview my father had given the *Rand Daily Mail* concerning the police charge against peaceful demonstrators on the opening day of the Treason Trial. Van den Bergh is now head of the Security Branch and my father not unreasonably fears that he will be seeking to punish me as quiet revenge for my father's earlier outspoken condemnation of the police. As well as being acknowledged as a fearless and effective advocate and the leading silk at the Johannesburg Bar, Maisels is a deeply observant Jew and has been president of the Jewish Board of Deputies, a man whom Yutar is bound to respect. He has agreed to help in securing my release.

I learn from my father that at the end of August or early September he had been granted an interview, at his request, with Vorster, the minister of justice. My father recorded the substance of this interview in a signed statement dated 21 November 1969. Although they were diametrically opposed politically, Vorster knew and respected my father. Vorster had been most cordial, and hypocritically said he was disgusted with the cowardice and weakness of the United Party opposition compared to the fearless stand of the Labour Party. He then opened his file and handed my father a copy of the transcript of my statement of 9 August. My father was left alone to read it. He recalled that 'there was nothing in the statement which incriminated any of the other detainees or provided information which could implicate anyone else'. Vorster's only concern was that youngsters at the 'liberal' English-language universities were exposed to the propaganda of communists 'like that Slovo' and he said he was determined to protect 'decent boys' from such 'evil influences'. My father then asked Vorster to release me from detention, since the Sabotage Act provided for the release of detainees who answered questions 'satisfactorily'. This Vorster refused, saying that he could not interfere with the attorney-general, who was preparing charges and 'justice will have to take its course', adding that the prosecution would be asking for the death penalty for those found guilty. He said that he had chosen 'an excellent and fair man' as prosecutor, Dr Yutar.

My father's second plea was that all 90-day detainees be allowed reading matter and writing material. Despite my father's arguments, Vorster remained adamant, claiming that the remedy lay in the hands of each detainee, who could end his detention by making a satisfactory statement – a claim contradicted by his refusal to authorise my release. The only concession he made

135

was to agree, now that I had made a statement, that I could be allowed the material to continue work that I was under contract to complete for the publishers Juta, to update *Gardiner and Lansdown's Criminal Law and Procedure.* He said he would instruct the commissioner of police to arrange this. In fact nothing happened for several weeks, and it was only towards the end of my detention that I received these materials. Without access to a law library it was impossible to do the work, but at least I had the massive two-volume *Gardiner and Lansdown* to read and annotate, so making my last few weeks in prison more tolerable. I learned later that, after representations by his employers, Festenstein had similarly been allowed medical books to complete his research.

My father and Maisels are clearly shocked by Vorster's statement that the prosecution will be seeking the death penalty. This is confirmed by what Yutar had said to me. I do not know if Yutar is simply carrying out orders from Vorster, or whether this is his own decision, but clearly Vorster wants his followers to see him as the 'man of granite' who is ruthlessly suppressing the extra-parliamentary opposition, and Yutar is determined to demonstrate the loyalty of the Jewish community. Maisels advises me that only if I agree to give evidence on the basis of my statement will he be able to persuade Yutar that I am genuinely on the fringes of the violent revolution planned by Mandela and the other leaders. He tries to reassure me that if I do so, I can still have a future as a lawyer in South Africa and cites the case of a well-known QC in Natal who had lived down a serious offence in his youth. My father says: 'You don't really have any alternative.' After these meetings, I am still hoping for an opportunity to consult my political comrades, whose advice will be crucial for me. So I tell Yutar that I am still undecided about his offer to indemnify me if I become a state witness. I naïvely fail to recognise that my uncertainty has handed Yutar the possibility of a publicity coup once I have been put on trial. Had I said yes at this stage, it might have been difficult for him to put me on trial.

I am taken back to Pretoria. The following day I am led into an office in the prison. One of the Security Branch men comes up to me and says: 'I hereby release you from detention.' My joy lasts only a split second because he immediately puts his hand on my shoulder and says: 'I am arresting you on a charge of sabotage. You will appear in court tomorrow.' One by one the other Rivonia men come into the room, are released from detention, and immediately arrested on charges of sabotage. I am standing near the door when Mandela is led in. He has been brought from Robben Island and has completed nearly one year of his five-year sentence. He is wearing khaki shorts, an open-necked shirt and ill-fitting open-toe sandals – the regulation garb for a black prisoner, humiliating for a professional man like Mandela. He looks quite different from the man to whom I said goodbye at the Old Synagogue 11 months earlier. He is now clean shaven and has lost about 30 pounds (13.6 kilograms); instead of his usual deep brown colour, his skin has a sickly, yellowish hue; in place of the rounded full face I remember, there are now hollow cheeks and bags under his eyes. But he still stands tall and straight-backed, and becomes his jovial, high-spirited self when he sees us all. He bursts into a big smile as he notices me and gives me a warm handshake, but he is obviously surprised to see me there. There is much excitement. For the first time in three months we can all talk openly to each other. Apart from Bernstein, Goldberg and Kantor, I have not seen any of the others since our arrest. Their disguises are gone, and they all look thinner and paler, but are thrilled to be reunited. I am shocked to see also among the accused Andrew Mlangeni and Elias Motsoaledi, who had been arrested some weeks before the Lilliesleaf raid. Mlangeni, a large strong man, repeats what he told me in the corridor waiting to see the magistrate, that he had been tortured with electric shocks and has the burn marks to prove it. I have known both him and Motsoaledi well for some years as active trade unionists, who had 'disappeared' about a year earlier, I presumed to go for military training.

We are soon joined by Joel Joffe, an attorney whom I know slightly from legal practice as a former partner of my cousin Fred Zwarenstein and James Kantor. With him are George Bizos and Arthur Chaskalson, both colleagues of mine at the Johannesburg Bar. They are part of the legal team that Fischer has put together to defend the accused. It is courageous of them to take on this case because there is already a large amount of hostile comment against the accused in the media. They will be ostracised by many in the white community, and can expect to be targeted by the police. They have been kept in the dark about when we will be charged. Having heard rumours that we are being released from 90-day detention, they have come to Pretoria and, with some difficulty, discovered that we were to be brought to court the following day, but they still do not know who is being charged and what the charges will be, whether sabotage or high treason or some other offence. When the lawyers arrived at the prison, the chief warder at first would not allow them to see the black and white accused together, but eventually on instructions from the commissioner for prisons he allowed this 'as an exception'.

I think that, at last, I will be able to get the guidance I badly need from my comrades about my situation. I announce immediately: 'I made a statement in detention, and Yutar wants me to be a state witness. I want to know what to do.' Bernstein and Goldberg already know about this. I spoke to Bernstein during our exercise period that morning. He said he could see no objection to my testifying along the lines of my statement, so long as I realised that this would end my future politically. He felt, however, that no one knew what effect 10 years or more of jail would have on someone, and we all knew that the death sentence was a real possibility. I mentioned to him the possibility of inducing Yutar to release me and then escaping. He thought this would be a good idea. When I raise the issue with the others at our first meeting, there is a silence. Joffe says that, as a lawyer for the defence, he cannot advise me whether or not to give evidence for the state, but that I should face the risks if I do not do so – a trial, a likely conviction and the probability of spending the rest of my life in jail or possibly even being hanged. He says that if I am still undecided, it would be better for me not to participate in any consultation with the other accused, and to be separately represented. At that stage I leave the room. I am later told that if I do stay in the trial, arrangements are being made for Michael Parkington, who was an attorney in the Treason Trial, to act for me and to instruct Sydney Kentridge, also a Treason Trial lawyer, as my counsel.

In court

Early the following morning, 9 October, we are handcuffed, loaded into a prison vehicle, whites at the front, black prisoners at the rear, and taken in a convoy of about 12 vehicles to the Supreme Court, a large, domed granite building overlooking Church Square in Pretoria. We are led by a number of cars carrying the head warder and high-ranking police officers, followed by riot trucks filled with uniformed police carrying Sten guns, batons, riot sticks and tear gas canisters. We are told 'this is the trial of the century and we are taking no chances'. Church Square is packed with armed police. The vehicles swing at speed through the iron gates into the back entrance of the Supreme Court and we are taken past lines of armed police through a series of gates into basement cells, one for the four white prisoners, another for the black ones. Goldberg, with his impish sense of humour, blocks the peephole in the door of our cell and says, 'Let's see what they do.' Within moments, police burst in with Sten guns at the ready, search us and warn us to keep the peephole unobstructed.

We are led up the steep stairs from the basement cells into the dock in G court on the ground floor. It is a large chamber in Victorian style with brown polished wood panels and seats and dark leather upholstery. I have been in this court before, but at the advocates' table, not in the dock. Mandela is Accused No. 1 and is the first to go up. I am Accused No. 11 and am the last to enter. I am seated in a temporary overflow dock alongside Mlangeni, with whom I am able to chat while we wait for the judge to arrive. I look around and see the strictly segregated public gallery is packed, the white section full of security policemen and our relatives, including my mother, who smiles and waves to me, and my father, who has a dejected expression below his deeply furrowed brow.

The judge enters. He is Quartus de Wet, judge-president of the Transvaal division of the Supreme Court, who announces that he will sit alone without assessors. (There are no jury trials in South Africa.) I have appeared before him as an advocate in two cases of murder and one of rape during my 18 months in practice at the Bar. The state provides *pro deo* (free) defence for anyone on a charge that carries the death penalty. Young advocates can earn five guineas a day and gain experience by undertaking this work – typically for South Africa, it is the most inexperienced lawyers whom black defendants get to defend them when facing the death penalty if they cannot afford their own lawyers. In one murder case, I persuaded De Wet to exclude a confession by the accused, which had not been signed in front of a magistrate, as required by the Criminal Code. Since this was the only direct evidence against the accused woman, who was alleged to have deliberately started a fire that caused the death of her two-timing boyfriend, I took the risky step of closing the defence case without calling the accused to testify. De Wet was annoyed by this tactic, but accepted that he had to acquit the accused owing to lack of evidence proving her guilt beyond reasonable doubt. In the other murder case, the accused was found guilty of murder, but De Wet readily accepted my plea of mitigating circumstances to avoid imposing the death penalty. In the rape case he was unsympathetic to a black schoolgirl who alleged that her black teacher had raped her, and summarily – in my private view, too readily – decided that there was no case to answer after I had cross-examined her. He could be obstinate and bad-tempered but generally dispensed rough justice. He did, however, share all the usual prejudices of white South Africans – I doubt whether he would have discharged in the same way a black defendant accused of raping a white girl.

Yutar stands up, crowing in his high-pitched voice: 'I call the case of *The State* vs *The National High Command and Others*'. He then hands the indictment to the judge and to the defence lawyers. This is the first time they have seen it, a lengthy, rambling and complex document alleging about 222 acts of sabotage committed between 1961 and 1963 as preparation for guerrilla war and an armed invasion of South Africa. Bizarrely, the National High Command, non-existent as a legal entity, is charged as a separate defendant. Mandela, Sisulu, Mbeki, Kathrada, Goldberg and Mhlaba are alleged to be members of a confusing list of bodies, the 'National High Command, the National Executive Committee of the National Liberation

Movement Umkhonto We Sizwe'. The other defendants, including me, are accused of being part of the overall conspiracy. James Kantor is charged in his own name and also as a partner in his law firm, an attempt to make him responsible for the acts of his partner, Harold Wolpe. Yutar hands in the attorney-general's authorisation that the trial be heard summarily without a preliminary examination. Bram Fischer QC, leading the defence for all the accused except Kantor and me, immediately stands up and asks for a four-week adjournment on grounds of the complexity and seriousness of the charges, and that the defendants have been in solitary confinement for three months and are in no condition to give instructions until they have a period for recuperation. Yutar objects and says two weeks will be sufficient (although the state has already had three months to prepare). The judge grants a three-week adjournment.

We are all buoyed up by the news that the UN General Assembly has demanded (by 106 to 1) that the trial should be abandoned and all the defendants released. We are world news and there are demonstrations in London, New York and elsewhere. My former teachers and senior colleagues at Wits University, professors HR (Bobby) Hahlo and Ellison Kahn, publicly condemn the UN resolution as 'an impertinent, unprecedented intervention in the domestic affairs' of an independent state. This is to be expected of Hahlo, a German refugee of Jewish origin who had converted to Christianity and is an ultra-conservative. He believes that blacks and women are not disciplined and experienced enough to master the intricacies of law, and had told Mandela he should not be studying at Wits. But it is surprising that Kahn, a liberal man and probably South Africa's greatest legal scholar, should associate himself with Hahlo's views. Kahn had inspired my belief, as a student in his constitutional law course, that the South African legal system fell far short of the Diceyan concept of the rule of law because of the arbitrary powers it gave to the executive over the black population, the legalisation of discrimination, and the severe restrictions on freedom of speech, association and movement. Now he is saying, with Hahlo, that in bringing to trial the Rivonia accused – who have been denied peaceful avenues to promote human rights and democracy – the South African government 'is acting in the best tradition of Western civilisation and in accordance with the rule of law'. Kahn's action shows just how frightened and keen to display their loyalty to the regime even liberal-minded whites have become.

Mandela's guidance

I am once again isolated from the other defendants and kept in a cell on the first floor of the prison, unable to converse with any of the other accused. Since I have not yet instructed lawyers, the only people I see, apart from warders, are members of my family, who are allowed to visit twice a week. On 16 October at my request I am able to attend a conference in the prison with Fischer and the other defendants, including Mandela. It is difficult to talk to the other accused because of the near certainty that the office in which we meet is bugged. Fischer tells me that their attitude and that of others in the movement outside is that I have to take a 'personal decision'. He says that I must realise that while they trust me, others might not be so forgiving.

I then talk to Mandela for some time, while standing next to a window so as to avoid being overheard. He says that if I actually testify, this might be used politically as a divisive measure against the ANC, but that he understands my predicament and I should take a personal decision. He says I will not be judged for the past, but rather by how I conduct myself in future. I ask what his attitude would be if I could persuade Yutar to release me conditionally, and then escape. He says: 'That would be excellent!' We shake hands and I leave.

Kantor and I are transferred to the Johannesburg Fort. We have separate cells but are allowed out into the yard together for lengthy periods. After the weeks of isolation in Langlaagte and Pretoria it is a relief to be able to talk to someone as entertaining and sympathetic as Jimmy. I feel deeply sorry for him. Yutar is punishing this innocent man by way of revenge for Wolpe's escape, and has even produced questionable evidence to prevent him being granted bail. Since he is not part of the underground organisations I do not reveal to him my secret plans.

The indictment under attack

On the morning of 29 October we are collected by the security police and taken to the Supreme Court in Pretoria. As we enter Church Square we see a large noisy crowd carrying placards: 'Free our Leaders'. We are taken to the cells below the court to join the other defendants and just after 10 am are led up the steep staircase from the cells. Mandela is again the first to enter the courtroom. I hear him shout out '*Amandla*' (Power), and the black audience responding enthusiastically '*Ngawethu*' (It shall be ours). Other defendants repeat this as they emerge from below. The many security police in the court are unable to prevent this demonstration of support. I am the last to enter the dock. Fischer launches an attack on the indictment. In his quiet, deliberate manner, with meticulous attention to detail, he exposes the many defects in the charges that have left the defendants in the dark about the case they have to meet. These include lack of particularity, confusion, obscurity and even allegations of acts committed before they had become unlawful. By the beginning of the second day of argument, it becomes clear that De Wet, who by now has put down his pen, is becoming impatient and annoyed with Yutar, for the mess he has made of the charges. Yutar is rattled as scorn is poured on his indictment. He has to find a distraction that will deflect public attention from his failings.

The moment of choice

At the tea break, I am taken up to Yutar's office. He says that he has decided to withdraw the charges against me, but will call me as a state witness. If he releases me now, will I promise to attend the hearing when called on to give evidence? The timing takes me by surprise. It is the moment of decision for me and I have only seconds to reply. Going rapidly through my mind is the fact that I have been promised, ever since I was induced to make a statement to the police explaining my presence at Lliesleaf, that I will be released, but they have broken that promise. In those circumstances I have no moral compunction in making a promise to Yutar that I know I will not keep – either I will escape the country, or if I cannot do so I will refuse to answer questions when put into the witness box. What I fail to appreciate in that flash of decision-making is that Yutar's unexpected timing of my release is part of a scheme to give him a publicity boost at the very moment that his indictment is thrown out.

I am taken back to court. As Dr George Lowen QC, Kantor's counsel, sits down after a withering critique of the indictment, De Wet turns to me. I am unrepresented. He asks whether I, too, wish to challenge the indictment. I stand up, but before I can reply, Yutar is on his feet: 'My Lord, I am withdrawing all charges against Advocate Bob Alexander Hepple,' dramatically adding, 'He will be the first witness for the prosecution.' The judge says, 'You may go.' The other accused, who are expecting this, appear to be unmoved. Mlangeni, sitting next to me, whispers: 'I'm glad you're getting out of this.' I rise and leave the dock, saying 'Good luck' to the other defendants. I am taken downstairs and released from custody. After nearly four months in custody I go home to my family. Joel Joffe provides a convincing explanation of Yutar's behaviour:

After that day's session, we sat over a coffee table discussing the reasons for Yutar's sudden move. He could have withdrawn the charge against Hepple earlier. Why did he wait until the judge forced Hepple into a position of speaking up? There was only one possible explanation. At the time it seemed far-fetched but it seemed to be so completely in keeping with Yutar's character as the case went on, that I have no doubt it is the right one. Yutar, on the one hand, hated Hepple with the kind of passionate hatred which he bore against all the accused and everybody connected with them. It was as though he had been personally wronged by them, and he was determined to bring them all to what he regarded as justice. He wanted Hepple as a witness, and was determined to use him, but he would punish him by leaving him in jail as long as he possibly could. The announcement of Hepple's defection was to be a masterstroke of publicity. I don't know at what stage of the case he had originally intended to announce it, but he had been faced with a crisis. Bram had virtually demolished the indictment. George Lowen had scorned it. The sentiment in court was running strongly against him. It was at this moment, when he knew that nothing he could say by way of reply could rehabilitate his indictment, that he decided the moment had come to save the face of the prosecution – and also his own face – and in doing so to steal some of the headlines from the evening newspapers if the indictment was rejected by the court.

The judge quashes the indictment. The accused are immediately re-arrested, a fresh indictment is presented and this time upheld, and the trial begins on 25 November. By then I am out of the country.

Preparing to escape

The police clearly do not believe that I am under any threat, and do not offer me protection, nor do I want a police presence. I tell a reporter on the day of my release that 'I feel too dazed to think clearly'. I decline to give any further press interviews. It is important not to give any hint that I am planning escape, so I return for a short time to practise at the Bar. I have to face the rather icy stares of other advocates as I enter the common room. One of the attorneys who used to instruct me corners me and shouts abusively that I am a 'fucking idiot' to have thrown away my career by working with Mandela. It is clear that my usual stream of work has dried up, but some individual colleagues are very supportive. Johann Kriegler (a judge of the Constitutional Court after 1994) is responsible for allocating *pro deo* briefs and he is generous in handing me a number of these. The day before we are due to escape I am engaged in a murder trial before Mr Justice Boshoff. I am anxious that it will not end in time, but fortunately, late in the afternoon after finding the accused guilty on the basis of strong evidence, the judge hears and accepts my plea of mitigating circumstances. I can leave with a clear conscience that I have fulfilled my professional duties.

On my release, I immediately make contact with Fischer, and we meet secretly for a whole Saturday morning in a hotel suite in the white suburb of Rosebank. This is a highly dangerous undertaking for us both. According to the rules of professional conduct, he should not be talking to a potential state witness. But I know that Fischer places his moral obligations to his 'family'

147

of political comrades above the rules he would strictly observe in an ordinary case. I am nervous, in case we are being watched, as I enter the suite that Fischer has arranged. He immediately puts me at my ease with his usual cheery smile and a warm handshake. He is deeply concerned about my predicament. He and Molly have given wonderful support to Shirley during my imprisonment. I tell him everything that has happened from the time of my arrest onwards. I propose to him that I should leave the country before I am called to give evidence. He puts the alternatives to me. The first is to give evidence so that I can be a 'friendly' witness for the defence when cross-examined. I reject that out of hand as politically and personally unacceptable. Ordinary people would not understand that ambiguous role. The second is to go into the witness box and refuse to testify. That might have the political advantage of embarrassing the prosecution, but would result in my going back into prison for contempt or for indefinite detention without trial or being re-indicted with Mandela and his colleagues. The final possibility is to flee the country as I propose. He wants to consult the defendants and other comrades.

We meet again one evening a few days later in another hotel suite. He tells me that they had spent more time discussing me than their own defence, and that they and others agree that I should leave the country. He says: 'We want to save you for the liberation movement.' I respond that I feel I have forfeited my position among the leadership, but I want to go on supporting the liberation movement in whatever way I can. We meet secretly one more time when he gives me the detailed plans for the escape. Eight days later Shirley and I make the hazardous journey described in the Prologue.

Yutar's revenge

When we arrive in Dar es Salaam, Tennyson Makiwane of the ANC meets us. He tells us that the South African police are now aware of our escape and that an angry and bitter Dr Yutar has told the court on Tuesday 26 November that I had fled the country because the Rivonia defendants and their supporters threatened me. In Joffe's words: 'Timed carefully to make the afternoon editions of the newspapers, Yutar announced in his most dramatic falsetto that his intended first witness, Advocate Bob Alexander Hepple, had been threatened by the accused or their supporters, and had fled the country.' At Makiwane's suggestion I immediately hold a press conference at Dar es Salaam airport. The *Tanganyika Standard* reported:

Mr Hepple said that allegations by Dr Yutar that he had been threatened were a complete fabrication. 'I have received no threats from any of the accused or anyone connected with them.' Mr Hepple said he had never received a subpoena to attend court as a prosecution witness although the prosecution had said he would do so. 'If I had gone into the witness box I would have had to refuse to answer questions.' … He said that the police had promised him that he would not be called as a state witness, that he would not be prosecuted and that he would be released from 90-day detention. On the strength of those promises he had made a statement to the police 'but this did not take the case against the accused any further'. All these promises had been broken and in the new charges against the other accused he had been named as a co-conspirator … 'It was clear to me that the State were [sic] trying to use me as a political tool … [The police] threatened that if I did not make a statement I

149

would be detained indefinitely and they would detain my wife.'

We are given a warm welcome by the senior ANC and SACP leaders, including Moses Kotane, Duma Nokwe and Joe Matthews, and the staff in their run-down offices in Independence Avenue. We give them a verbal report on the Rivonia arrests and trial, and convey a number of messages from Fischer. 'We are glad to have you,' says Kotane, 'you are still the Bob we used to know.' But I encounter a different attitude from some of the white London exiles. I meet Michael Harmel, Joe Slovo and Vella Pillay. Harmel delivers a lecture telling me that I have not behaved like a 'good communist'. He is a deeply committed communist, and the Party's leading theoretician. But, as Turok has remarked, 'on the human level, he could be cruel with a streak of vindictiveness, particularly with those who strayed from the party line'. I lose my temper and say that he is no position to tell anyone how to behave in view of his own shocking record in security matters. I say that the blame for the Lilliesleaf arrests rests on his shoulders and that of others who had behaved recklessly. Some days later Slovo and Pillay ask me for a written report on all that has happened. I refuse on the ground that I do not trust their security. Nor do I think there is any more to say beyond what I had reported to Fischer in South Africa and to the leaders in Dar. However, I give them a full verbal report. At the end of this I say that I have lost confidence in the Party leadership and they seem to have lost confidence in me. I tender my 'resignation', but they respond that there is no provision for this in the Party constitution. They both remain warm, friendly and sympathetic.

I had not anticipated the revenge that Yutar would seek. I was to be his first, star witness. Although I had said nothing that would take the state case any further, he was hoping to make political capital out of the fact that I would speak as one who was a colleague of the accused, an officer of the court, and the son of a distinguished political opponent of the regime. Now I was gone and had stated publicly that I would never testify against the accused, whom I respected and admired. The first intimation of Yutar's plans, aided and abetted by the notorious Swanepoel, to discredit me among my former colleagues came at the end of January 1964 when Swanepoel testified about information he falsely alleged I had given the police. Then on 23 April Yutar cross-examined Sisulu and asked him if he classified me as a 'traitor'. Sisulu replied that he did not know what I had said to the police. Yutar then referred him to Swanepoel's evidence. Sisulu said that if that evidence were true, then he would consider me to be a traitor. Perhaps predictably, the media incorrectly reported that Sisulu had said that I was a traitor.

I felt a deep sense of shock as I read this report in the next morning's *Times* while travelling to work on the London Underground. My mother recorded in a statement, dated 26 November 1969, that late on the night of 23 April Bram and Molly Fischer unexpectedly arrived on the doorstep of my parents' home in Johannesburg. Their purpose was to ask my parents to get a message to me as quickly as possible, that Sisulu had been trapped in cross-examination into making his statement, and he wanted me to know that these were not his real feelings. Fischer himself was extremely perturbed that this statement had been wrung from Sisulu and he repeated again and again to my parents that he and the accused had the highest regard for my integrity, and wanted me to know this without delay. When my parents told Molly and Bram that they had received letters from Shirley and me saying that we had been badly treated by a few of the leading white South African refugees in London, Bram was most upset and said: 'They must be mad.'

I wrote a strong letter of protest to Joffe, the defence attorney. He responded that Sisulu was most upset that his answers, given under the pressure of cross-examination, had been taken out of context. Sisulu sent me a personal handwritten letter, which was delivered to me in London by Vella Pillay on 25 May, setting out the true position.

My dear Bob,

I have authorized my attorney to reply to you and to give you the full facts of what actually happened. But at the same time I felt that I should personally write to you about this matter. Even before we received your letter, we had made some efforts to convey to your father the true position; but owing to our difficulties and pressure of work in the case it was not possible to do this in time. We were not only concerned about the effect this would have on you, but about your parents as well, who not only are personal friends to some of us, but whom we hold in very high esteem.

I sincerely very much regret the publicity given to my evidence by the press on this matter and the inconvenience which must have been caused by this affair. It certainly did not reflect my views about you. Apart from the facts that the statement was taken out of its context, I was forced to answer a question put to me by Dr Yutar...

Unfortunately, the press reports had done their damage. An underground publication *Freedom Fighter* gave the real names of Mr X (Bruno Mtolo) and Mr Y (Patrick Mtembu), who had given evidence for the state at the trial. The pamphlet also named

> My dear Bob,
>
> I have authorized my attorney to reply to you and to give you the full facts of what actually happened. But at the same time I felt that I should personally write to you about this matter. Even before we received your letter, we had made some efforts to convey to your father the true position; but owing to our difficulties and pressure of work in this case it was not possible to do this in time. We were not only concern about the effect this would have on you, but about your parents as well, who not only are personal friends to some of us, but whom we hold in very high esteem.
>
> I sincerely very much regret the publicity given to my evidence by the press and the inconvenience which must have been caused by this affair. It certainly did not reflect my views about you. Apart from the facts that the statement was taken out of its context, I was forced to answer a question put to me by Mr Yutar.

me as a 'traitor'. In the 'Little Rivonia' trial, on 14 December 1964, David Kitson, one of the members of the new National High Command of MK, testified that his fellow member Wilton Mkwayi (whom I had known as a leading trade unionist), had been upset by the opinion of *Freedom Fighter*. 'He did not regard Hepple as a traitor and said that he was reflecting the general African opinion on this. It was thought that Hepple's name had been put in only to give a multi-racial flavour to a list which would otherwise have been all black.'

Parting ways with the SACP

Slovo contacted me after the *Freedom Fighter* appeared. He wanted to assure me that I was not regarded as a traitor and that the statement had not been authorised. The people who had put my name on the leaflet obviously did not know the facts. A few weeks later he asked to meet me and said that the London bureau had recommended my expulsion from the Party and the Central Committee in exile had confirmed this. He again assured me that I was not considered to be a traitor but merely that I had been guilty of an 'error of judgement' in making a statement to the police, and in allowing Yutar to make a public announcement that I was to be a state witness.

There was another reason for my exclusion which Slovo did not mention, but which I discovered many years later. In 1990 Joel Joffe talked to some members of the ANC and then wrote to me:

> I said I could not understand why more sympathy had not been shown towards you, that in my view you had always been totally committed to the ANC, and what it stands for, and I thought it unfair that you should be treated in this way. From the responses that emerged I gathered that the problem was not your involvement in the Rivonia trial but had something to do with political activities in which you had been involved prior to that trial.

I never discovered exactly which activities they had in mind, but I suspect that these leaders had heard that I had helped to organise a discussion group of dissidents, most of them black comrades, which had produced some internal papers highly critical of the Party. The group had started in 1959 and went out of existence in March 1960 because of the state of emergency. The fact is that I had no wish to continue as a Party member. I had been distant from the SACP's pro-Soviet stance for a long time, and was disturbed by the direction the armed struggle was now taking, in particular Operation Mayibuye. The reckless goings-on at Lilliesleaf had thoroughly demoralised me. Any contribution I could make to the anti-apartheid struggle would be outside the ranks of the Party. I refrained from any public attack on the Party and kept silent.

I believe that I acted with integrity and loyalty to those with whom I had worked in South Africa when I took the personal decision to seize the opportunity to escape from the Rivonia Trial, and to leave the SACP. But the Party's decision to turn this into an expulsion for my 'error of judgement' meant not only political death for me but also social ostracism so far as a few of the hardline white communists in exile were concerned. This was particularly tough for Shirley and her parents, whose only fault was to have remained loyal to me. But our real friends and family gave us the support we needed to survive and start a new life.

I have often reflected on the difference between communists like Fischer and others like Harmel. Although I may have disappointed Fischer, a model of selfless dedication and personal sacrifice, by not staying on trial, he respected my dignity and autonomy, told me to make a 'personal' decision and helped me to escape. Harmel, on the other hand, reflected the Stalinist view that personal interests must always be subordinated to the 'collective' interests of the organisation and that no sacrifice is too great. In the words of Liu Shaoqi, notes from whose book *How to Be a Good Communist* were found in Mandela's handwriting at Lilliesleaf, 'every Party member must completely identify his personal interests with those of the Party both in his thinking and in his actions'. Mandela, a selfless revolutionary like Fischer, respected me as an individual who should make a 'personal' decision.

Banned and smeared

I still had to contend with the security police. Yutar delivered one last blow against me. In his closing speech in the trial he mockingly 'nominated a shadow cabinet for the provisional revolutionary government'. Coming to me, he said: 'From the information that Bob Hepple has given the police I would like to make him Minister of Information. But because Bernstein already occupies that post, I name Bob Hepple Minister of Informers instead.' Gordon Winter, a former agent for the Bureau of State Security, later claimed that Hendrik van den Bergh had instructed him in 1963 'to mount a smear alleging that [Hepple] had been a security police informer'. In 1966 the government showed that it still regarded me as a dangerous subversive by putting me on a list of banned members of unlawful organisations. I remained banned until 3 February 1990, at the time of Mandela's release. One of the consequences of the ban was that nothing I wrote or said could be quoted in South Africa. Ellison Kahn even thought it necessary to get permission from the minister of justice to quote in the *South African Law Journal* from an article which I had written on the law of negotiable instruments in 1961, and which had been approved by the Appellate Division of the Supreme Court!

Mandela: the matter is closed

The last word on this topic belongs to Mandela. In his unpublished prison memoir he comments on the publicity given to Sisulu's evidence concerning me. He writes: 'We were aware that during his detention Bob, after consultation with two of the accused, had made a statement to the police which was considered to be innocuous, the idea being that he would be discharged and able to flee the country.' He then describes Sisulu's evidence, and says that Yutar's allegation about the information I had given 'was received by us with reservations as the prosecution would readily make such an allegation as a retaliatory act against a man who has outwitted them. After the press publicity relating to this we received a strong protest from Bob reminding us that the whole idea of his making a statement and leaving the country had been discussed and he strenuously refuted the allegation made by Yutar. We accepted his assurance and as far as we are concerned the matter is closed.'

A lucky man

In June 1964 Mandela, Sisulu, Mbeki, Mhlaba, Kathrada, Goldberg, Mlangeni and Motsoaledi were found guilty. Bernstein was found not guilty and was discharged. Kantor had been discharged at the end of the state's case because there was no prima facie evidence against him. When sentencing those convicted, De Wet said that in essence the main crime of conspiracy was one of high treason, but since the state had not charged the crime in this form, he would not impose the death penalty. Thirty years later, Yutar claimed that he had deliberately charged sabotage and not treason so as to avoid a death penalty. But this is a curious justification, because sabotage also carried the death penalty and there can be little doubt that Yutar's reason for preferring this charge was that it was easier to prove. Yutar's claim is also contradicted by what he told me, and what Vorster told my father. I do not believe that De Wet – who in my experience was not a 'hanging' judge – took instructions from Vorster, but he was sufficiently politically astute, as Vorster was, to recognise that the eyes of the world were on South Africa and death sentences would be likely to precipitate world-wide sanctions. He sentenced them all to life imprisonment. The brilliance of Fischer and the other defence counsel also ensured that they were not sentenced to death.

Sadly, Fischer was himself sentenced to life imprisonment in 1966 and died of cancer, still a prisoner, in 1975.

It is idle to speculate whether I would have been convicted had I stayed on trial. I had made a statement that contained admissions of supporting the other accused, although not as a member of MK. Bernstein, who had admitted in his evidence that he had visited Lilliesleaf on various occasions as an architect, managed to persuade the judge that he was not part of the conspiracy. However, Kathrada, against whom the evidence was almost equally slender, was found guilty. Norman Levy concludes: 'the evidence against Ahmed Kathrada and Raymond Mhlaba was as slender as the case against Hepple, yet they each received life sentences'. Even if I had been acquitted on the conspiracy charges, I would have been found guilty of membership of an illegal organisation. I consider myself to be a lucky man to have escaped from the trial.

EPILOGUE

9 July 1996

Buckingham Palace

There was a queue of guests at the state banquet waiting to be presented by Her Majesty The Queen to the first democratically elected President of the Republic of South Africa. When my turn came, the greeting was not a decorous handshake. Mandela exclaimed: 'Bob, is that you?' and embraced me with a great bear hug. It was a lovely moment, full of joy and gratitude and redemption. And in that moment of intense feeling both Mandela and I rather overlooked the smallish woman who was standing slightly to one side with her hand outstretched. As we walked away my wife, Mary, pointed out that the Queen was still waiting for me to acknowledge her. When I told this story the next day to a senior judge, he jokingly threatened to send me to the Tower for *lèse-majesté*. But I have it on good authority that Her Majesty did not mind a bit because of her high regard for Mandela. Sometimes there are more important things than protocol.

I had sat with my mother in Canterbury, England on 11 February 1990 to watch the live TV broadcast of Mandela walking free out of Victor Verster prison after 27 years'

159

incarceration. We shed tears of joy. Sadly, my father, who had devoted his life to fighting for democracy and human rights and been forced into exile, was no longer alive. My mother had died by the time I watched Mandela inaugurated as president in 1994, one of those rare moments, in Seamus Heaney's words, 'when hope and history rhyme'. During the state visit in 1996, Mendi Msimang, the South African high commissioner, invited a number of South African expatriates including me to his residence in Kensington to meet Mandela. Mandela said to us: 'Whenever I meet black South Africans, they say to me: "We have had a great victory." Whenever I meet white South Africans they say: "Nothing much has changed." They are both wrong. We have made a great historical compromise. No one has won. We have agreed to live together in a democratic state in which the rights of all our people, white and black, are protected.' The ideals of democracy and human rights, for which so many thousands had suffered, died, been imprisoned or exiled, had triumphed.

July 1990
Return to South Africa

At the time of Mandela's release from prison, the banning orders imposed by the South African government which prevented me from returning to South Africa were lifted. I immediately received an invitation to a labour law conference in Durban in July 1990. I was on my way from Geneva to Windhoek, as an expert of the International Labour Organisation (ILO), to draft a labour code for the newly independent Republic of Namibia. The ILO was still enforcing UN sanctions against South Africa, so I had to take a four-day break in my contract with the ILO, to address the conference. I chose as my topic, 'The role of trade unions in a democratic society'.

The white Nationalists were still in power, and returning refugees were always uncertain whether or not they would be detained. As I nervously stepped into the arrivals hall at Johannesburg, watched over by Sten-gun-carrying soldiers and their dogs, a voice over the PA system said, 'Professor Hepple, wherever you are, stand still and put up your hand!' I froze, thinking the worst. Then a young Afrikaner woman approached me and said, 'Professor, your friend Professor Dugard is here to fetch you.' John Dugard and I had met as graduate law students in Cambridge in 1964. I had followed a career as an academic and practising lawyer in Britain, while he had returned and, as an international human rights lawyer, had bravely used legal processes as a form of 'politics by other means' against the apartheid government. He drove me past the house in Bezuidenhout Valley where I was born, and then across the new, unfamiliar highways to a much-expanded Wits University, before I set off for Durban. There I was warmly greeted by old trade union and lawyer friends who had survived imprisonment and banning orders, and I made contact with a new generation of labour lawyers. I already knew some of them as students who had attended my course on international and comparative labour law at University College London in the 1980s. These and other lawyers had creatively used labour and human rights law, in the dying days of apartheid, to assist the growth of the unions that played a decisive role in bringing about change. Shirley, my partner through the years of exile, joined me on this first emotional visit back to South Africa. But it was to be our last together. We separated in 1991. I married Mary Coussey in 1994.

During my years as an exile, I was inspired by Mandela's parting words to me: 'You will be judged, not by the past, but by how you conduct yourself in the future.' I had avoided imprisonment but wanted to keep on working for democracy in

161

South Africa. I kept out of exile politics and no longer had any role in the Congress movement, but I was an energetic member of the anti-apartheid movement at local level, helping to found branches in Cambridge and Canterbury. I helped my parents, who had set up the information service for the International Defence and Aid Fund, and later became a trustee of the Canon Collins Trust, supporting refugees and other southern African university students at universities. In April 1991 I presented the Labour Code I had drafted for Namibia to President Sam Nujoma. I was pleased to have the opportunity to contribute to the South Africa's framework of human rights when I was asked to join the ministerial task force set up by the minister of labour, Tito Mboweni, to draft the new Labour Relations Act (enacted in 1995). This enabled me to apply for the benefit of the country of my birth some of the expertise I had developed as a legal scholar and practitioner during 30 years on the international and European scene. The University of the Witwatersrand, whose senior law professors had publicly disowned me in 1963, conferred on me an honorary doctorate of laws in 1996, as did the University of Cape Town in 2006. I became an honorary professor of law at UCT, a fellow of the Stellenbosch Institute for Advanced Study, and a regular visiting lecturer at Wits and other South African universities.

1963–2013

Human wrongs into human rights

I came to appreciate, after settling in Britain in 1964, that the struggle for equality is not confined to one country, but is a fundamental part of the universal struggle for human rights. This was brought home to me when I was sent by the Anti-Apartheid Movement to address a branch meeting of the Transport and General Workers' Union (TGWU) at Willesden Bus Depot. I spoke of the hardships suffered by black South African workers and their unions, the discriminatory labour laws, and the racist theory that white workers must be protected from black competition. There was warm applause, a vote of solidarity, and a promise of support for the Anti-Apartheid Movement. To my surprise the very next item on the agenda was a motion, which was unanimously carried, opposing the employment of 'coloured immigrants' in London Transport. After the meeting, my hosts invited me to the local pub. I asked them how they could reconcile this motion with their opposition to racial discrimination in South Africa. The response was one that I had heard all my life in South Africa from white workers: 'These people are coming to take our jobs and will bring down our wages.' In South Africa these attitudes had been fortified over three centuries by ideas and practices of racial superiority. In Britain, white Labourites generally claimed that they were not racist, but they were deeply affected by the lingering attitudes of the imperial age. I soon appreciated that the attitudes and behaviour that I thought I had left behind in South Africa were commonplace in Britain. 'No Coloureds, No Irish, No Dogs' were notices that could be seen in landladies' windows. White workers went on strike to protest against the employment of black workers. Retail managers turned away non-white jobseekers on the ground that their customers would not like to be served by them.

The similarities between the racism I had been involved in fighting in South Africa and that in Britain led me to become involved in community relations and the anti-discrimination movement in Britain. It also led me to propose to the Cambridge Law Faculty, where I had enrolled for a postgraduate degree in English law in 1964, that my dissertation should be on racial discrimination and the law in Britain. Learned professors told me that the topic was unsuitable because there was, at the time, no law on the subject. It was precisely because of the absence of anti-discrimination law that I wanted to find out why the wrong of racial discrimination was not being legally remedied. Only Dr Paul O'Higgins, a teacher of labour law and public law in Cambridge, expressed enthusiasm and supervised the research that led to *Race, Jobs and the Law in Britain* (1968, second edn 1970). This was the first book of its kind and was influential in the framing of the Race Relations Act 1968, the Sex Discrimination Act 1975, and the Race Relations Act 1976

While working as a lecturer in law at the University of Nottingham between 1966 and 1968 I joined the Nottingham Commonwealth Citizens Consultative Committee. I was able to learn at first hand from local residents about the massive discrimination they suffered in housing and jobs. As chair of the employment committee I went to see several large employers, who simply denied the existence of racial discrimination, until a survey by an independent research organisation showed that it was widespread. This was fuel to our campaign for the Act of 1968, which for the first time outlawed racial discrimination in employment. In the 1980s I served on the Commission for Racial Equality, the independent agency charged with promoting equality and enforcing the law against discrimination. In 1997, I came together with others in a campaign to persuade the Labour government to create a single Equality Act and single Equality and Human Rights Commission for Great Britain, covering all strands of status discrimination. We undertook a substantial independent review of the enforcement of equality legislation. The report I wrote with Mary Coussey and Tufyal Choudhury was described by the leader of the House of Lords as the 'firm foundation' on which the single Equality Act 2010 was based.

Discrimination is still an issue throughout Europe, nowhere more so than in the case of the Roma, Europe's most persecuted minority. In 2001 I was asked to chair the European Roma Rights Centre (ERRC), based in Budapest. This organisation has successfully used litigation under the European Convention on Human Rights as a basis for protecting Roma people against police brutality, forced removals, segregated schooling and compulsory sterilisation. This experience persuaded me that a similar international organisation was needed with the task of promoting equality as a fundamental human right. I supported the remarkable Bulgarian activist Dimitrina Petrova, who previously directed the ERRC, in setting up in 2007 the London-based Equal Rights Trust, which now works in over 25 countries around the globe promoting legislation and other measures to advance equality.

The other major branch of my academic and practising life over the past 50 years has been international, European and British labour law. My trade union background and sympathies made it almost inevitable that I would develop this specialisation, and my experience in two different legal systems gave a comparative angle to my research. The subject is a meeting point of socioeconomic, political and human rights perspectives. As my expertise in this field developed, I became involved in work for the European Commission, participating in drafting European Union (EU) employment protection measures, and acted as an ILO expert. The last-mentioned role included a mission in 1992 to advise the post-communist Russian Federation on labour relations. I was amused by graffiti on a sculpture of Karl Marx opposite the Bolshoi Theatre on which the words (in Russian) 'Workers of all countries, Unite!' had been replaced by 'Workers of all countries, Forgive me!' This just about summed up my feelings as we learned more and more about what had been done in the name of Marx in the Soviet Union.

In my lifetime I have been fortunate to witness the transformation of many terrible human wrongs into human rights, from the horrors of the Holocaust into a system of international human rights law, from Nazism, fascism and Soviet-style communism into pluralist political democracy, from apartheid to a South African constitution which entrenches equality and human rights under the rule of law. Yet, racial and gender oppression have not been eliminated from the face of the earth, detention without trial and torture are still routine in many countries, and authoritarian regimes continue to suppress the freedom of association, free speech and dissent. One may also ask how much nearer the human rights movement has brought poor and disadvantaged people to social and economic justice. The old ideas of state socialism and communism, now dead, envisaged a political, economic and social transformation of society. Social democracy has not yet succeeded in reconciling capitalism and social justice. Inequality between rich and poor is growing both internationally and nationally, and the recently liberated South Africa is no exception.

Human rights have been described by the historian Samuel Moyn as a form of 'minimalism', which replaces the 'maximal' issues of transformation. This is part of the attraction of human rights because, as Mandela recognised, it makes political compromise feasible. But human rights now face a crisis as attempts are made to extend them beyond the political and civil sphere to social and economic rights, and from formal equality to transformative equality. In the eyes of critics on the right, the promotion of socioeconomic rights is simply discredited social democracy or, worse, socialism through the back door. Critics on the left argue that the individualism implicit in human rights undermines the notions of solidarity and collectivism on which social justice is based.

Mandela and his comrades who launched the failed revolution in the early 1960s did not have the luxury of debating such questions. Their priority was to overthrow a brutal racist regime by whatever means were available. They never deluded themselves that the underground struggle for democracy would be short or easy but they were ill prepared for the predictable, violent response by the apartheid regime. This had tragic consequences for many South Africans who were tortured, imprisoned and forced into exile. There followed nearly 30 years of intensified violence and repression, but these years also saw the emergence of new democratically based movements such the resurgence of trade unionism in the 1970s and the United Democratic Front in the 1980s. The key to large-scale social change now lies in non-violent political processes grounded in law. People have to take ownership of their hard-won rights and participate actively in their realisation rather than simply expecting the state to deliver them. Three essential features of those processes are an independent judiciary, a free press, and democratic trade unions and social organisations. Human rights are not a 'last utopia' but are essential weapons in the eternal struggles of the powerless against the powerful, a struggle in which human rights activists and lawyers have a vital role.

The heroic sacrifices of Mandela and countless others whose names are not now remembered remind us, in Mandela's words, that 'there are few misfortunes in this world that you cannot turn into a personal triumph if you have the iron will and the necessary skill'. Whatever setbacks we experience, each one of us can make a contribution, in our own way, to equality, human rights, and social justice.

WHO'S WHO†

Family

Coussey, Mary Winifred (*née* **Dowding**) (born in Plymouth, 11 September 1943). Second wife, married 6 April 1994. Daughter of Stanley and Winifred Dowding. Mother of Harriet Mary Edwards (born 6 October 1978) and Christopher James Edwards (born 7 February 1981). Worked for Race Relations Board and as a director of Commission for Racial Equality, independent race monitor of Immigration Service, chair Advisory Board for Naturalisation and Integration, immigration detention centre monitor, awarded CBE for services to community relations 2007.

Hepple, Agnes (*née* **Borland**) (1871–1960). Paternal grandmother. Born on the farm Mielietuin, Weenen county, Natal, on 26 October 1871, daughter of Alexander Borland (born Ayrshire, Scotland, 1837), a blacksmith, who settled in Natal in 1855, and Marie Theresa Coyle (born in County Cork, Ireland, 1840). At the age of 20 she left Pietermaritzburg to live with an aunt in Johannesburg, where she married Thomas Hepple in

† It has not been possible to find biographical details of all the individuals mentioned in this book. The main sources are SA History online (www.sahistory.org.za), Karis and Carter, 1972, and the biographies listed in the Bibliography.

1896. They had seven children, five of whom survived infancy, including Alex. She died in Johannesburg January 1960.

Hepple, Alexander (Alex) (1904–83). Father. Born in La Rochelle, Johannesburg, 28 August 1904, third child of Thomas and Agnes. Left school at age of 14, worked as office boy and qualified at night school as chartered secretary. Married Josephine (Girlie) Zwarenstein (below) 3 October 1931. Became manager of her family's business until 1951 when he resigned to devote himself to political activity. Lifelong member of SA Labour Party, elected to Transvaal Provincial Council 1943, and to Parliament for Rosettenville constituency (1948–58). Elected leader Labour Party 1953. Chairman Treason Trial Fund and Defence and Aid Fund, editor (with Girlie) of *Forward*, Labour newspaper, until government measures forced its closure. Moved to England 1965 and set up International Defence and Aid Fund's information service, wrote *Verwoerd* (Pelican, 1967) and *South Africa: A political and economic history* (Pall Mall, 1967). Died in Canterbury, 16 November 1983.

Hepple, Josephine (Girlie) (*née* **Zwarenstein**) (1906–92). Mother. Born in Braamfontein, Johannesburg, 21 January 1906, elder daughter of Alexander and Jacoba Zwarenstein. Went to Teachers' Training College and became a primary school teacher in Elsburg 1925. Married Alex Hepple on 3 October 1931. She worked part-time in family business, ran Alex's election campaigns, worked as his researcher and, after his defeat in 1958, was joint editor of newspaper of Garment Workers' Union and of *Forward*. After coming to England she set up IDAF information service with Alex. Died in Canterbury, 24 October 1992.

Hepple, Shirley Rona (*née* **Goldsmith**) (born Volksrust, 21 July 1932). First wife married 7 July 1960, two children Brenda (born 7 July 1961) and Paul Alexander (born 11 December 1962), separated 1991, marriage dissolved 1994. Daughter of Minnie and Morrie Goldsmith, political activists. Attended Pretoria Girls' High school. Member SACOD. Worked as personal assistant to Shulamith Muller, attorney in political and union cases. After coming to England was citizens advice worker.

Hepple, Thomas (Tom) (1869–1944). Paternal grandfather. Born in Sunderland, England, 26 June 1869, son of Thomas Hepple (born 1849) and Margaret Hutchinson (born 1852). After apprenticeship as patternmaker, emigrated to Johannesburg in 1893, married Agnes Borland 1896. They were founding members of SA Labour Party in 1908, and he was secretary of Jeppestown branch of Amalgamated Society of Engineers, blacklisted by employers for participation in 1913 strike. Died in Johannesburg in June 1944.

Monasch, Bertha (1909–87). Cousin of Girlie and Dolly. Born in Rotterdam 10 April 1909. Her parents, Pinas Monasch (born 1873) and Hester (*née* Zwarenstein, born 1870), and aunt Mietje, both sisters of Alexander Zwarenstein, died in Auschwitz 15 October 1942. Bertha at first escaped deportation because she was married to Jan van Dam, a Christian, but had to go into hiding in February 1944. She died in Amsterdam 24 March 1987.

Zwarenstein, Alexander (Oupa) (1877–1942). Maternal grandfather. Born in Zuid-Beijerland, Netherlands, 25 January 1877, eighth of 10 children of Samuel Zwarenstein (1834–

1919) and Sprientje Monasch (1835–1918). Emigrated to Johannesburg 1898, opened butcher's shop, joined Boer forces in Anglo-Boer war, after which built up wholesale meat business (Azet Products). Married Jacoba Esther Schaap, four children, Samuel (1904–61), Victor Alexander (1912–78), Josephine and Dorothy. Died in Johannesburg 30 June 1942.

Zwarenstein, Dorothy (Dolly) (1908–94). Aunt and 'other mother', sister of Girlie. Born in Johannesburg 23 April 1908. First member of family to obtain university degree, taught at Rosettenville junior school and became principal of Belgravia junior school. Spent 1939 as exchange teacher in London and helped to evacuate children at start of war. One of the founders at Mayibuye night schools for Africans in 1940; left South Africa in 1966 and worked as remedial teacher in Chelmsford before retiring to live with Girlie in Canterbury, where she died on 5 July 1994.

Zwarenstein, Fred. Lawyer. Son of Simon Zwarenstein (brother of Alexander). Cousin of Girlie and Dolly.

Zwarenstein, Jacoba Esther (*née* **Schaap**) (1883–1935). Maternal grandmother. Born in Orange Free State, South Africa, April 1883; married Alexander Zwarenstein 26 August 1903, four children, died 5 March 1935.

Zwarenstein, Sprientje. Daughter of Solly Zwarenstein (brother of Alexander), cousin of Girlie and Dolly.

Political activists
Anderson, Joan (born 1934). Teacher. Member SLA, SACOD and FEDSAW, blacklisted by government when teaching

at Central Indian High School, left country during state of emergency 1960.

Bernstein, Lionel (Rusty) (1920–2002). Architect. Joined CPSA in 1938, secretary Labour League of Youth, founder member of SACOD and principal drafter of the Freedom Charter. Member of the SACP Central Committee, arrested at Lilliesleaf 11 July 1963. Acquitted in subsequent Rivonia Trial and escaped while on bail on other charges in 1964 with his wife Hilda to Botswana and England.

Cachalia, Ismail Ahmed (Maulvi) (1908–2003). Muslim priest. Member SAIC, participant in 1946 passive resistance campaign, deputy volunteer-in-chief Defiance Campaign 1952, ran 'freedom transport' (with Babla Saloojee), fled to Botswana 1964 and set up ANC office in New Delhi. Brother of Yusuf Cachalia.

Cachalia, Yusuf (1915–95). Secretary of SAIC, tried and given suspended sentence in Defiance Campaign trial 1952, banned continuously from 1953, and under house arrest. Brother of Maulvi Cachalia.

Carneson, Fred (1920–2000). Journalist and business manager *Guardian* and *New Age*, arrested over 60 times, Treason trialist, member Central Committee SACP, imprisoned in 1964 for seven years.

Feinstein, Charles Hilliard (1932–2007). Economic historian. Chair SLA and SACOD youth branch, left South Africa 1954, became fellow and senior tutor of Clare College, Cambridge, and Chichele Professor of Economic History, Oxford.

Festenstein, Hilliard (H) (1930–89). Immunologist. Arrested when he arrived for MK committee meeting at Lilliesleaf 11 July 1963 and detained under 90-day law. Found guilty of furthering the activities of the SACP and possessing banned literature, but this was overturned on appeal in 1964 and he joined his wife Iris and family in England.

First, Ruth (1925–82). Journalist *Guardian* and *New Age*, and author. Member of SACP central committee, fled to Swaziland during 1960 state of emergency, Treason trialist, detained without trial in 1963 and left for England after her release. Killed by South African Police parcel bomb while working in Mozambique in 1982. Married to Joe Slovo.

Fischer, Abram (Bram) (1908–75). Born into prominent Afrikaner family, won Rhodes scholarship to Oxford, became advocate at Johannesburg Bar and Queen's Counsel. Joined CPSA in 1938. Member of SACP Central Committee, led defence (with Israel Maisels QC) in Treason Trial (1956–61), and in Rivonia Trial (1963–64). Arrested for sabotage and communist activities, he jumped bail and went underground, was captured in 1965 and sentenced to life imprisonment. He died from cancer in 1975. Married to Molly Fischer (1908–64), also a political activist, who died in a car accident soon after the end of the Rivonia Trial.

Goldberg, Denis (born 1933). Engineer. Member of SACOD, SACP and MK. Arrested at Rivonia 11 July 1963 and sentenced to life imprisonment. Released 1985.

Goldreich, Arthur (1929–2011). Artist and designer. Born in South Africa, joined Palmach, military wing of Jewish National

Movement in Palestine. Returned to South Africa in 1954, designed sets for *King Kong*, the African musical. Member of SACP and MK, lived with family at Lilliesleaf Farm. Arrested 11 July 1963, escaped from Marshall Square police station 11 August with Harold Wolpe and two others, by promising bribe to warder. Settled in Israel and worked as architect.

Kasrils, Ronald (Ronnie) (born 1938). Member SACP and founding member MK, escaped from South Africa to Tanzania with partner Eleanor in 1963, worked underground for ANC in South Africa, became minister of water affairs and minister of intelligence.

Harmel, Michael (1915–74). Joined CPSA in 1939, one of the two members of the Central Committee (the other was Bill Andrews) who voted against dissolution of the Party in 1950, became a full-time functionary and leading member of the underground SACP from 1953. He was sent abroad in 1963, and worked for *World Marxist Review* in Prague.

Kantor, James (1927–74). Lawyer. Brother-in-law and partner in legal practice of Harold Wolpe. Detained in 1963 after Wolpe's escape and charged but acquitted in Rivonia Trial and left South Africa.

Kathrada, Ahmed (Kathy) (born 1929). Leading member of the TIC and SAIC, joined Young Communist League aged 12, member of the SACP central committee, Treason trialist. After frequent bannings, arrests and house arrest, went underground in April 1963, arrested at Rivonia 11 July 1963 and sentenced to life imprisonment. Released in 1989, elected MP in 1994, and served as political adviser to President Mandela.

Kitson, Ian David (1919–2010). Mechanical engineer and draughtsman. Born in South Africa, worked in England after war service until 1959 when he returned to South Africa with wife Norma. Member SACP and MK, became member of High Command MK after Rivonia arrests. Arrested in October 1964, sentenced to 20 years' imprisonment for sabotage and membership of SACP.

Kotane, Moses (1905–78). Joined ANC in 1928 and CPSA in 1929, full-time Party and trade union functionary from 1931, studied in Moscow for one year. He was general secretary of CPSA and of its successor SACP from 1939, and treasurer-general of ANC 1963–73. Went into exile in 1963 and died in Moscow after long illness.

Levy, Leon (born 1929). Trade unionist, member of SACOD and SACP, president SACTU (1955–63). Treason trialist acquitted (1961), first person detained under the 90-day detention law in 1963; went into exile in England after his release. Twin brother of Norman Levy.

Levy, Norman (born 1929). Teacher, university professor. Member of SACOD and SACP, Treason trialist, detained and tortured in 1964, sentenced to three years' imprisonment for membership of SACP, then banned. Went into exile in England. Twin brother of Leon Levy.

Mandela, Nelson Rolihlala (born 1918). Lawyer. Member ANCYL and ANC 1943, Transvaal president and national volunteer-in-chief Defiance Campaign 1952. Arrested and tried for treason with 156 others 1956, detained under state of emergency 1960, after acquittal in Treason Trial went underground and led stay-at-home against declaration of white republic 1961. Co-founder (with Joe Slovo) and first commander-in-chief of MK, went abroad for five months in 1962 for military training and to gather support from other African countries, arrested 5 August 1962 and sentenced on 7 November to five years' imprisonment for incitement and leaving country unlawfully. Indicted as Accused No. 1 in Rivonia Trial October 1963, sentenced to life imprisonment, released 11 February 1990, elected first president of democratic South Africa (1994–99). Married first (1944–58) to Evelyn Ntoko Mase with whom he had four children, married second (1958–96) to Nomzamo Winnie Madikizela with whom he had two daughters, married third to Graça Machel (1998).

Marks, John Beaver (JB) (1903–72). Trade unionist and leader of African Mineworkers strike 1946, Transvaal president of ANC, chair of SACP, deployed to join external mission of ANC in Tanzania 1963.

Mbeki, Archibald Mvuyelwa Govan (1910–2001). Teacher, trade union organiser, journalist and author. Joined ANC in 1935 and SACP in 1953, member of SACP Central Committee, ANC national executive, and High Command of MK. Went underground November 1962, arrested at Rivonia 11 July 1963, and sentenced to life imprisonment. Released from Robben Island 1987. Elected deputy-president of Senate (1994–97) and its successor, the National Council of the Provinces (1997–99). Father of Thabo Mbeki (president of South Africa, 1999–2008).

Mhlaba, Raymond (1920–2005). Trade unionist, joined ANC 1944, volunteer in Defiance Campaign, continuously banned, member of the SACP Central Committee, ANC national executive, and of MK High Command. Arrested at Rivonia 11 July 1963 and sentenced to life imprisonment. Released 1989, became premier of the Eastern Cape 1994.

Mkwayi, Wilton Zimasile (1923–2004). Trade unionist, member SACP and ANC, a leader of the Defiance Campaign in the Eastern Cape, Treason trialist, and MK commander-in-chief after Rivonia arrests, sentenced to life imprisonment in 'little Rivonia' trial in 1965. Released 1989. Elected to national Senate and Eastern Cape legislature.

Mlangeni, Andrew Mokete (born 1926). Trade unionist, active in bus boycott and strike in 1955, joined ANCYL in 1951, member of SACP, ANC and MK, sent for military training in 1962, arrested on his return and sentenced to life imprisonment at Rivonia Trial in 1964. Released 1989.

Molete, Zachius Botlhoko (born 1930). Member national executive PAC, acting president PAC 1960–2, sentenced to three years' imprisonment in 1963 for furthering aims of PAC, fled to Lesotho while on bail pending appeal, and acted as PAC representative in East Africa.

Mothopeng, Zephania (Zeph) (1913–90). Teacher. Joined ANCYL 1943. President PAC 1959, jailed for two years for incitement after Sharpeville massacre, detained without trial and tortured in 1963, banished and banned, detained after Soweto uprising, sentenced to 15 years' imprisonment in 1979. Released 1988.

Motsoaledi, Elias (1924–94). Trade unionist, joined ANC 1948, continuously banned from 1952, member SACP and

MK. Sent for military training in 1962, arrested on return and sentenced to life imprisonment at Rivonia Trial in 1964. Released 1989.

Ndzanga, Lawrence and his wife, **Rita** (born 1933) were active in the Railway Workers' Union and SACTU. He died in January 1977 in police custody, having been detained without trial since November 1976. Rita was also detained and tortured, and banned. She became a patron of FEDSAW and a member of the democratic Parliament.

Nokwe, Philemon Pearce Dumasile (Duma) (1927–78). First black advocate admitted to Bar. Member ANC, secretary-general from 1958, Treason trialist, deployed to external mission of ANC in Tanzania 1963.

Paton, Alan (1903–88). Author, teacher, principal Diepkloof Reformatory (1935–48), a leader of the Liberal Party (1953–68).

Sachs, Albert Louis (Albie) (born 1935). Lawyer and author. Student activist, participated in Defiance Campaign 1952, defended in political trials, member SACOD, detained twice without trial, banned, went into exile. Blown up by South African police bomb in Mozambique, losing arm and eye. Judge of Constitutional Court (1994–2009).

Saloojee, Suliman (Babla) (1932–64). Member SAIC, one of the 'Picasso club' that painted slogans, ran 'freedom transport' (with Maulvi Cachalia). Died on 9 September 1964 two months after being detained under 90-day law, having allegedly jumped from 7th floor of security police headquarters, but probably murdered by interrogators.

Shall, Sydney (born 1932). Research scientist. Volunteer in Defiance Campaign 1952, member SLA and SACOD, Treason trialist, left country during state of emergency 1960.

Sibande, Gert (1907–87). 'Lion of the East', leader of farmworkers, member of ANC, exposed farm labour scandals and led potato boycott 1959, Treason trialist, banished to Komatipoort, went into exile.

Sisulu, Walter Ulyate Max (1912–2003). The 'father of the struggle' who turned ANC into militant mass movement, joined ANC in 1940, met Mandela in 1941 and with him founded ANCYL in 1944, elected secretary-general of the ANC 1949. Joined SACP in 1953 after five-month visit to communist countries. After frequent banning orders, arrests and house arrest went underground in April 1963. Member of SACP Central Committee, ANC national executive, and MK High Command. Arrested at Rivonia 11 July 1963 and sentenced to life imprisonment. Released 1989 and became deputy-president of ANC. Married to Albertina Sisulu (1918–2011), nurse and ANC activist, 'the mother of the nation'.

Slovo, Joe (1926–95). Lawyer. Joined CPSA in 1942, studied law at Wits, and became advocate at Johannesburg Bar; under banning orders from 1954. Member of SACP Central Committee and co-founder with Mandela of MK. Left South Africa in June 1963, became member of ANC national executive, chief of staff of MK and general secretary of SACP. Minister of housing in Mandela government 1994. Married to Ruth First.

Sobukwe, Robert Mangaliso (1924–78). University teacher. Member of ANC until he helped found PAC in 1958. Arrested after Sharpeville massacre 1960 and sentenced to three years' imprisonment, but kept as prisoner on Robben Island until 1969 under specially enacted legislation, then placed under house arrest in Kimberley, where he qualified as a lawyer but died of cancer.

Turok, Ben (born 1927). Member SACOD and SACP, founding member MK, sentenced in 1962 to three years' imprisonment for sabotage. Went into exile 1966 and became MP after 1994.

Weinberg, Eli (1908–81). Trade unionist and photographer. Born in Latvia where he was imprisoned for political and union activities. Came to South Africa in 1929 and joined CPSA in 1932. Married first to Ray Alexander (Simons) and second to Violet Weinberg. Repeatedly banned, arrested in 1964 and sentenced to five years' imprisonment for membership of SACP Central Committee after Rivonia arrests, banned on release and obtained political asylum in Tanzania.

Wolpe, Harold (1926–96). Lawyer and sociologist. Student activist, member SACP and MK, as lawyer arranged purchase of Lilliesleaf Farm and acted in political cases. Arrested 1963 while trying to flee after Rivonia raid, escaped 11 August from Marshall Square police station with Arthur Goldreich and two others, and fled to England where he was joined by his wife AnnMarie and children. He worked as a university lecturer in sociology. Returned to South Africa in 1990, and worked in the University of the Western Cape. Father of Nicolas Wolpe, founder and director of the Lilliesleaf Trust.

Organisations

African National Congress (ANC). Formed as the South African Native National Congress in 1912, renamed ANC in 1923. Banned by the government following the state of emergency in March 1960 and went underground until the ban was lifted in 1990. Became governing party after first democratic elections on 27 April 1994.

African National Congress Youth League (ANCYL). Founded in 1944 by Mandela, Sisulu, Tambo and others, to counter the ANC's conservative policies, and to promote civil disobedience and strikes. Banned from 1960 to 1990.

Communist Party of South Africa (CPSA). See South African Communist Party.

Congress alliance. Formed in 1950s between ANC, SACOD, SACPO, SACTU and SAIC, on the basis of the Freedom Charter adopted at the Congress of the People held at Kliptown, 26 June 1955.

Federation of South African Women (FEDSAW). Formed 1954 as non-racial women's movement organising anti–pass campaigns, including a march in Pretoria of 20,000 women on 9 August 1956.

Liberal Party of South Africa (LPSA). Founded 1953, open to all racial groups. Supported qualified franchise, bound members to use only constitutional and democratic means. Dissolved 1968 after legislation prohibited multi-racial political organisations.

National Party (NP). Founded 1914 by Afrikaner nationalists. Formed government, led by General JBM Hertzog under pact with SALP 1924–9, united with South African Party to form United Party in 1933. Afrikaner nationalists led by Dr DF Malan formed 'Purified' National Party, which became governing party pursuing apartheid policies from 1948–94, with JG Strijdom, Dr HF Verwoerd, BJ Vorster, PW Botha and FW de Klerk as successive leaders. Disbanded in 2004.

Pan Africanist Congress (PAC). Founded as breakaway from ANC in 1959, led by Robert Sobukwe under slogan 'Africa for the Africans'. Anti-pass campaign culminated in Sharpeville massacre on 21 March 1960. Banned 1960–1990.

South African Coloured People's Organisation (SACPO). Formed 1953 as organisation of people of mixed race, part of Congress alliance, dissolved in exile 1966.

South African Communist Party (SACP). Formed in 1921 as CPSA, which was dissolved by Central Committee in 1950 in anticipation of banning under Suppression of Communism Act 1950. Reformed as SACP in 1953 and became legal in 1990. Part of the Congress alliance.

South African Congress of Democrats (SACOD). Formed 1953 by white radical supporters of ANC, part of Congress alliance. Banned 1962.

South African Congress of Trade Unions (SACTU). Formed 1955 as only multi-racial trade union federation after dissolution of SA Trades and Labour Council, part of Congress alliance. Following bannings and arrests of leaders 1963–4 established external mission. Succeeded by Congress of SA Trade Unions (COSATU) from 1985.

South African Indian Congress (SAIC). Founded 1923 following foundation of Natal Indian Congress (NIC) by MK Gandhi in 1894, and also comprising Transvaal (TIC) and Cape congresses. Organised passive resistance campaign 1946, became member of Congress alliance. Never banned but crippled by state repression from 1963.

South African Labour Party (SALP). Founded in 1908 mainly by British immigrants; formed pact government with NP 1924–9 and had electoral pact with Smuts's United Party 1943–53. After 1948 adopted non-racial policies but lost all parliamentary representation in 1958, after which it was dissolved.

Umkhonto weSizwe (MK). 'Spear of the Nation' formed in 1961 with Mandela as first commander-in-chief, merging with military units of SACP and becoming autonomous military wing of ANC. Launched sabotage campaign 16 December 1961. Disbanded 1994 and merged with SA Defence Force.

United Party (UP). Ruling party 1934–48 supported white minority rule, formed by merger of Hertzog's NP and Smuts's South African Party. Led by Hertzog until 1939, then by General JC Smuts until 1950.

Note on Sources

I have relied extensively, especially in chapters three to seven, on notes I made in May and June 1964, a few months after my escape from South Africa, while the events were still fresh in my mind. An edited version of part of these notes under the title 'Rivonia: The story of accused No. 11' was published in *Social Dynamics* (2004). Other parts of my notes on the underground during 1960–3 have never been published.

There appears to be no official record of Mandela's 1962 trial (chapter two) because this was held in a special regional magistrate's court and not the Supreme Court. I have been able to use press cuttings and a timeline kindly supplied to me by the Nelson Mandela Foundation, as well as Mandela's own accounts (1976, 1994), a compilation of speeches and evidence by the International Defence and Aid Fund (Mandela, 1978), and the typewritten text of Mandela's closing speech, corrected by him and me, and related correspondence, which I found serendipitously in the archives of IDAF held at the Mayibuye Centre, University of the Western Cape. In relation to the Rivonia raid and trial I have utilised an extensive collection of press cuttings assembled by my late mother, Girlie Hepple, as well as archive materials and recorded interviews held by the

Liliesleaf Trust, Rivonia, personal correspondence, and the authoritative account of the trial by Joffe (1995, 2007). I have also referred to memoirs, biographies and histories, including those in the Bibliography.

A full bibliography of my writings, and recorded interviews regarding my career, may be found in the Eminent Scholars Archive: http://www.squire.law.ca.ac.uk/eminent_scholars/.

Bibliography

Benson, M (1989) *A Far Cry: The making of a South African*, Viking, London

Bernstein, H (1967) *The World That was Ours*, Heinemann, London

Bernstein, R (1999) *Memory against Forgetting*, Viking, London

Bizos, G (2007) *Odyssey to Freedom*, Random House, Houghton

Brown, KS (2012) *Saving Nelson Mandela: The Rivonia Trial and the fate of South Africa*, Oxford University Press, New York

Bundy, C (2012) *Govan Mbeki*, Jacana, Johannesburg

Bunting, B (1998) *Moses Kotane South African Revolutionary: A political biography*, Mayibuye Books, Cape Town

Clingman, S (1998) *Bram Fischer: Afrikaner revolutionary*, David Philip, Claremont

Dyzenhaus, D (1998) *Judging the Judges, Judging Ourselves*, Hart Publishing, Oxford

Ellis, S (2012) *External Mission: The ANC in exile 1960–90* C Hurst & Co., London

Feinstein, C (2005) *An Economic History of South Africa*, Cambridge University Press, Cambridge

Goldberg, D (2010) *The Mission: A life for freedom in South Africa*, STE Publishers, Johannesburg

Hahlo, H and Kahn, E (1960) *The Union of South Africa*, vol. 5 in the series (ed. Keeton) *The British Commonwealth: The development of its laws and constitutions*, Stevens, London

Hepple, A (1966) *South Africa: A political and economic history*, Pall Mall, London

Hepple, A (1967) *Verwoerd*, Penguin, London

Hepple, A (1984) *The South African Labour Party 1908–58: A memoir* [online] www.sahistory.org.za

Hepple, B (1990) The role of trade unions in a democratic society, *Industrial Law Journal* [South Africa], **11**, 645–54

Hepple, B (2004) Rivonia: The story of accused No. 11, *Social Dynamics* [UCT], **30** (1), 193–217

Hepple, B (2011) *Alex Hepple: South African socialist*, South African History Online, Cape Town [online] www.sahistory.org.za

Hepple, B (2011a) *Equality: The new legal framework*, Hart Publishing, Oxford

Hirson, B (1995) *Revolutions in My Life*, Witwatersrand University Press, Johannesburg

Joffe, J (1995) *The Rivonia Story*, Mayibuye Books, Cape Town

Joffe, J (2007) *The State vs Nelson Mandela: The trial that changed South Africa*, Oneworld Publications, Oxford

Kantor, J (1967) *A Healthy Grave*, Hamish Hamilton, London

Karis, T and Carter, G (1972) *From Protest to Challenge: A documentary history of African politics in South Africa 1882–1968*, vol. 4: *Political Profiles*, Hoover Institution Press, Stanford, CA

Kasrils, R (2010) *The Unlikely Secret Agent*, Jacana, Johannesburg

Kathrada, A (2004) *Memoirs*, Zebra Press, Cape Town

Lerumo, A [Michael Harmel] (1971) *Fifty Fighting Years: The South African Communist Party 1921–1971*, Inkululeko Publications, London

Levy, N (2011) *The Final Prize: My life in the anti-apartheid movement*, South African History Online, Cape Town [online] www.sahistory.org.za

Lodge, T (2006) *Mandela: A critical life*, Oxford University Press, Oxford

Luckhardt, K and Wall, B (1980) *Organise or Starve: The history of the South African Congress of Trade Unions*, Lawrence and Wishart, London

Maharaj, M (ed.) (2001) *Reflections in Prison*, Zebra, Cape Town

Mandela, N (1976) [accessed 6 March 2012] *Prison Memoir* [online] www.nelsonmandela.org

Mandela, N (1978) *The Struggle is My Life*, International Defence and Aid Fund, London

Mandela, N (1994) *Long Walk to Freedom*, Little, Brown, London

Mandela, N (2010) *Conversations with Myself*, Macmillan, London

Meer, F (1988) *Higher than Hope: A biography of Nelson Mandela*, Hamish Hamilton, London

Mendelsohn, R and Shain, M (1998) *The Jews of South Africa: An illustrated history*, Jonathan Ball, Cape Town

Meredith, M (1997) *Nelson Mandela*, Hamish Hamilton, London

Meredith, M (2002) *Fischer's Choice: A life of Bram Fischer*, Jonathan Ball, Cape Town

Moyn, S (2010) *The Last Utopia: Human rights in history*, Bellknap Press and Harvard University Press, Cambridge, Mass., and London

Müller, M (1998) *Anne Frank: The Biography*, Henry Holt, New York

Murray, B (1997) *Wits: The 'open' years*, Witwatersrand University Press, Johannesburg

Pogrund, B (1990) *Sobukwe and Apartheid*, Rutgers University Press, New Brunswick

Sampson, A (1999) *Mandela: The authorised biography*, HarperCollins, London

Sargant, W (1959) *Battle for the Mind*, Pan Books, London

Simpson, AWB (1992) *In the Highest Degree Odious: Detention without trial in war-time*, Clarendon Press, Oxford

Sisulu, E (2002) *Walter and Albertina Sisulu: In our lifetime*, David Philip, Cape Town

Slovo, J (1995) *Slovo: The unfinished autobiography*, Ravan Press, Johannesburg

Smith, DJ (2010) *Young Mandela*, Weidenfeld and Nicholson, London

South Africa Truth and Reconciliation Commission (1998) *Truth and Reconciliation Commission of South Africa Report*, vol. 2: *Repression and resistance*, Truth and Reconciliation Commission, Cape Town

Strydom, L (1964) *Rivonia: Masker af!*, Voortrekkerpers, Johannesburg

Turok, B (2003) *Nothing but the Truth: Behind the ANC's struggle politics*, Jonathan Ball, Cape Town

Winter, G (1981) *Inside BOSS: South Africa's secret police*, Penguin, London

Wolpe, A (1994), *The Long Way Home* David Philip, Claremont

Acknowledgements

Members of my family and several friends have read all or part of earlier drafts, put me right on facts and helped to clarify and improve expression. In particular I am grateful to Mary Coussey, Maureen Donnelly, Brenda Henson, Paul Hepple, Shirley Hepple, Joel Joffe, Norman Levy, Terry Moore, Joan Shall and Sydney Shall. Fran Shall's copy-editing has greatly improved my drafts. I received much encouragement and advice from Frances Wilson and from speakers and colleagues at her stimulating masterclass in 2012 on writing the 'new' biography. I alone am responsible for the opinions expressed, and any mistakes that remain.

I also wish to thank the following for their generous help in finding archival sources: Adrienne van den Heever and Nic Wolpe of the Liliesleaf Trust; Verne Harris, Lucia Raadschelders and Sahm Venter of the Nelson Mandela Foundation; Graham Goddard and Geraldine Frieslaar of the Mayibuye Centre at the University of the Western Cape. Nic Wolpe's support in publishing this book has been crucial.

Acknowledgements are made to Joel Joffe for the quotations in chapter seven from *The State* v *Nelson Mandela* and from his correspondence with me. I am indebted to those who have allowed me to use their photographs.

All royalties after expenses will go to the Liliesleaf Trust.

Index